Incredible Odisha
Celebrating the Rhythms and Traditions of Odisha

Incredible Odisha
Celebrating the Rhythms and Traditions of Odisha

Dr. Sonali Sahu

BLACK EAGLE BOOKS
Dublin, USA | Bhubaneswar, India

Black Eagle Books
USA address:
7464 Wisdom Lane
Dublin, OH 43016

India address:
E/312, Trident Galaxy, Kalinga Nagar,
Bhubaneswar-751003, Odisha, India

E-mail: info@blackeaglebooks.org
Website: www.blackeaglebooks.org

First International Edition Published by
Black Eagle Books, 2025

INCREDIBLE ODISHA
(Celebrating the Rhythms and Traditions of Odisha)
by **Dr. Sonali Sahu**

Copyright © Dr. Sonali Sahu

All rights reserved. No part of this publication may be reproduced, stored in a retrieval system, or transmitted, in any form or by any means, electronic, mechanical, photocopying, recording or otherwise without the prior permission of the publisher.

Cover & Interior Design: Ezy's Publication

ISBN- 978-1-64560-712-0 (Paperback)

Printed in the United States of America

I dedicate this book to my
beloved mother Urmila Sahu,
whose love, strength and endless encouragement
have been the foundation of my dreams.
This book is a reflection of your blessings.

CONTENTS

Foreword	09
Introduction to the Incredible Odisha	13
Odishi Dance of Odisha: A Timeless Tradition of Grace and Spiritual Expression	15
Goti Pua Dance: The Living Tradition of Odisha's Cultural Heritage	21
Chhau Dance of Mayurbhanj: Odisha's Martial Dance Tradition	26
Danda Nacha: The Sacred Folk Dance of Ganjam, Odisha	32
Bagha Nacha: The Vibrant Dance of Ganjam, Odisha	37
Sambalpuri Dance: The Rhythmic Soul of Sambalpur's Cultural Heritage	41
Dhemsa Dance: The Tribal Rhythm of Odisha's Koraput Region	47
Laudi Khela of Jajpur: A Cultural Gem of Odisha	53
Pala Nacha: The Traditional Dance-Drama of Odisha	58
The Juang Dance of Keonjhar: A Vibrant Expression of Tribal Culture and Tradition	63
Dalkhai Dance of Jharsuguda: A Celebratory Tradition of Odisha	66
Devdasi Dance of Odisha: A Sacred Tradition of Grace and Devotion	70
Ram Leela of Ganjam District: A Vibrant Celebration of Tradition and Devotion	75
Ravana Chhaya: The Shadow Play of Odisha	80
Jamera Ghoda Nacha: The Dance of the Decorated Horse from Bolangir	83
Mawla Jhula: The Swing Festival of Bargarh	86
Jhumar Dance: The Folk Rhythms of Balasore	89
Mugala Tamasa: The Satirical Folk Theater of Bhadrak	92
Ghanta Patua: The Traditional Storytelling Art of Cuttack	96

Prahalad Natak: The Spiritual Folk Drama of Ganjam	100
Paika Akhada: The Martial Dance Tradition of Gajapati	104
Jhipa Nacha: The Ritualistic Dance of Jajpur	109
Bull Dance of Kendrapara: A Unique Folk Art	113
Kela Keluni Nata: The Traditional Folk Drama of Khordha	117
Malkangiri Changu Dance: A Vibrant Folk Tradition of Odisha	122
Koya Dance of Nabarangpur: A Celebratory Folk Tradition of Odisha	127
Kaleshi Dance of Nayagarh: A Traditional Folk Dance of Odisha	132
Lariha Dance of Nuapada: A Traditional Folk Dance of Odisha	137
Rayagada Lanjia Soura Dance: A Glimpse into Tribal Culture	142
Sonepur Mayala Joda: A Unique Tribal Dance of Odisha	145
Domkach of Sundargarh: A Vibrant Tribal Dance of Odisha	149
Jodi Sankha of Ganjam: A Symbol of Tradition and Devotion	153
Radha Prem Leela: The Divine Love Play of Ganjam District	159
Rayagada Paraja Saura Dance: A Vibrant Celebration of Tribal Culture and Devotion	163
Chadheya Dance of Ganjam: A Folk Symphony of Love, Nature, and Social Awakening	166
Ghumura Dance of Kalahandi: A Vibrant Expression of Tribal Culture, Heroism, and Social Unity	170
Ghudki Dance: A Rhythmic Reflection of Western Odisha's Cultural Soul	174

Foreword

Odisha, the land of temples, traditions, and timeless tales, is equally a land of dance—where every gesture tells a story and every rhythm echoes centuries of devotion, resistance, joy, and cultural identity. In this vibrant landscape, dance is not merely an art form but a way of life—deeply rooted in ritual, religion, and rural expression. Incredible Odisha is a celebration of this remarkable cultural inheritance, unfolding through the myriad folk and classical dance forms that have flourished in different districts across the state.

At the heart of Odisha's classical dance heritage lies Odissi, one of India's oldest surviving dance forms, born in the sanctum of temples and refined through centuries of spiritual practice. Once nurtured by Devadasis—temple dancers dedicated to divine service—Odissi embodies spiritual expression through sculptural grace and abhinaya (expressive storytelling). The tradition of Gotipua, where young boys dress as female dancers to carry forward the rituals and stories once told by Devadasis, adds another layer of resilience and continuity to Odisha's classical legacy.

Parallel to this sacred elegance is the robust vibrancy of Odisha's folk and tribal dances, which reflect the pulse of its people. Chhau, with its martial movements and stylized masks, tells mythological stories through athletic grace and powerful expression, particularly in regions like Mayurbhanj and Keonjhar. Danda Nacha, observed during the Chaitra month, merges penance, devotion, and performance into a spiritual spectacle, where devotees offer their bodies in service of Shiva.

The western districts of Odisha bring forth a riot of color and rhythm through forms like the exuberant Sambalpuri dance, the communal Dhemsa of the tribal heartlands, and the graceful Jhumar, often performed during harvests and festivals. Dal Khai, popular among the women of western Odisha, celebrates feminine energy and festivity, while the lesser-known Laur Khalsa adds a unique martial flair to devotional celebration.

Storytelling takes center stage in traditions like Pala, Moghal Tamsa, and Rama Leela, where music, dialogue, and movement come together in open-air stages to keep epic narratives alive. In Ravana Chhaya, the rare shadow puppet theatre of Odisha, myth meets minimalism in a hauntingly beautiful format that is both visual and oral.

The coastal belts and central districts give us dynamic forms like Ghoda Nacha, where men dress as horse riders in mock battles or celebratory processions, and Ghana Patua, where acrobatic and tantric elements merge in springtime worship. From the ritual drama of Prahlad Natak, which enacts the tale of Vishnu's Narasimha avatar, to the vigorous tradition of Paika Akhada, which preserves martial arts heritage and community pride, Odisha's cultural canvas is both deep and wide.

Through this book, Incredible Odisha, meticulously prepared by Dr. Sonali Sahu, an effective teacher in English and an efficient scholar with in-depth knowledge on cultural nuances, we invite readers to explore these traditions not as isolated performances but as living legacies tied to the land, the festivals, the faiths, and the everyday lives of its people. Each dance form is a mirror to the region's history, its resilience, and its connection to the divine and the communal.

We owe a deep debt of gratitude to the artists, gurus, scholars, and communities who continue to breathe life into these traditions. It is their passion and perseverance that have inspired this book. May this work serve as a step toward preserving, documenting, and celebrating the diverse dance heritage of Odisha.

Let us move together to the rhythm of Incredible Odisha.

Prof. Basanta Kumar Panda
Project Director
Centre of Excellence for Classical Odia
Ministry of Education
Govt. of India
Email:panda.bk@rediffmail.com

Introduction to the Incredible Odisha

As I sit down to pen the words of this book, The Incredible Odisha, I am deeply touched by the richness and vibrancy of our cultural heritage. Odisha, a land of timeless beauty, is not just known for its breathtaking landscapes, temples, and traditions, but also for its folk dances, which are the soul of its people. Through this book, I seek to explore and celebrate the diversity of Odisha's folk dance forms, one from each district, reflecting the unique identity and spirit of the regions they hail from.

Growing up in Odisha, I was always surrounded by the enchanting sounds of the dhol, the rhythmic beats of tribal drums, and the mesmerizing footwork of traditional dances. These dances, passed down through generations, hold the stories of our ancestors and are a reflection of our values, our connection with nature, and our belief systems. As I traveled across the districts of Odisha, witnessing these dance forms in their raw, unfiltered glory, I felt a profound sense of pride and reverence for the rich cultural tapestry that binds us together as a people.

The decision to write this book stems from my desire to preserve and share these folk dances with the world. In a rapidly changing world, where traditional art forms often struggle to survive, I feel a deep responsibility to document and celebrate them. These dances are more than just performances; they are living expressions of Odisha's cultural diversity, and through them, we can connect with our roots, our history, and our future.

My motive behind this book is simple yet profound: to bring to light the lesser-known yet incredibly rich folk traditions of Odisha and to rekindle pride in our cultural heritage. Each district of Odisha tells its own story through its dance, and I hope that by sharing these stories, I can inspire others to appreciate, protect, and promote our folk traditions. My goal is not just to record these dances but to encourage future generations to keep them alive, ensuring that they continue to flourish for years to come.

As you turn the pages of The Incredible Odisha, I invite you to take a journey with me through the diverse cultural landscape of our state. Let us celebrate the dance, the music, the spirit, and the soul of Odisha—a state that continues to inspire, enchant, and connect us all to our shared heritage.

Dr. Sonali Sahu
(The soul belongs to the soil of Odisha)

Odishi Dance of Odisha: A Timeless Tradition of Grace and Spiritual Expression

Odishi, also known as Odissi, is one of the classical dance forms of India that originated in the state of Odisha. With its roots deeply embedded in ancient traditions and religious practices, Odissi is a unique and graceful dance form that combines intricate footwork, expressive gestures, and captivating storytelling. This dance form is not just an art; it is an embodiment of spirituality, culture, and heritage, passed down through centuries. Odissi holds a significant place in India's classical dance tradition and is renowned for its graceful movements, sculptural poses, and elaborate technique.

Origins and Evolution

Odissi has its origins in the temples of Odisha, where it was performed as Mahari dance (devotional dance by temple dancers) dedicated to Lord Jagannath and other deities. Initially performed as a form of temple dance to worship the gods, it later evolved into a classical dance form with more structured elements. It was practiced as part of religious rituals and ceremonies in the temples of Odisha, particularly the famous Jagannath Temple in Puri.

The dance form is known for its distinct style, which involves tribhangi (a three-fold bending of the body), graceful fluid movements, intricate footwork, and expressive hand gestures (mudras). The performance includes the use of classical ragas (melodies) and talas (rhythms), which are integral to Odissi's enchanting appeal.

Key Elements of Odissi Dance

Odissi involves a combination of chandanas (ritualistic poses), foot stamping, torso movements, and elaborate hand gestures that convey a range of emotions. It is characterized by a delicate balance of angular poses and fluid movements, often described as a visual poetry of the body.

1. Mudras: Hand gestures play a central role in Odissi, helping to express meanings, emotions, and narratives. Each mudra or gesture tells a story and adds to the storytelling aspect of the performance.
2. Tribhangi: This is a fundamental posture in Odissi, where the dancer bends at three points — neck, torso, and knee. It is considered the ideal pose of grace, creating a sculptural and symmetrical look.
3. Footwork: The footwork in Odissi is intricate and rhythmic, with a focus on precision and control. Dancers often perform on the squared or lotus position, making the feet's movements a vital part of the performance.
4. Expressions: Odissi dancers use facial expressions to convey emotions. The Abhinaya (expression) is a crucial element that communicates the mood and the essence of the music, be it devotion, love, or joy.

The Mahan Gurus of Odissi

Odissi has been shaped and enriched over centuries, particularly by several key figures or Mahan Gurus who played pivotal roles in preserving and reviving this art form. Their contributions have elevated Odissi to an international stage. Here are some of the most prominent gurus in the history of Odissi dance:

1. Padmavibhushan Guru Kelucharan Mohapatra (1926–2004)

Guru Kelucharan Mohapatra is regarded as one of the most significant figures in the revival of Odissi. A legendary dancer, choreographer, and teacher, he is credited with giving a contemporary dimension to Odissi while preserving its traditional essence. He revolutionized the dance form by introducing it to the stage and making it accessible to the wider world. His contributions to Odissi have made him an icon in the dance community, and his disciples continue to carry his legacy forward.

2. Padma Bhushan Guru Protima Gauri (1946–1999)

Guru Protima Gauri was a renowned dancer and one of the leading exponents of Odissi. She is famous for her innovative approach to Odissi, combining classical techniques with modern sensibilities. Guru Gauri was instrumental in bringing Odissi to national recognition and was a respected educator who trained many successful Odissi dancers. She is often credited for introducing Odissi dance to international audiences.

3. Guru Ratikant Mohapatra (b. 1963)

Guru Ratikant Mohapatra, the son of Guru Kelucharan Mohapatra, is a renowned Odissi guru in his own right.

He has performed across the globe and is known for his mastery of the classical techniques of Odissi. As a teacher, he has played a key role in the transmission of the art form to the next generation, founding the Srjan Dance Academy in Bhubaneswar to promote and teach Odissi.

4. Guru Madhavi Mudgal (b. 1954)

Guru Madhavi Mudgal is one of the leading figures in the world of Odissi, celebrated for her graceful movements, profound understanding of music, and dedication to the tradition. A disciple of Guru Kelucharan Mohapatra, she has performed extensively in India and abroad and is known for her elegant style and precise technique.

5. Guru Kelu Charan Mohapatra

Guru Shrimati Kelu Charan Mohapatra was a prominent figure in the classical dance tradition, instrumental in the study and teaching of the Odissi style. His contributions were significant in ensuring that Odissi remained relevant in contemporary times while retaining its cultural and historical roots.

6. Guru Gangadhar Pradhan (1930–2013)

Guru Gangadhar Pradhan was one of the leading exponents of Odissi in the 20th century. He made significant contributions in the areas of both the performance and the theoretical aspects of Odissi. His approach to dance choreography emphasized the importance of body control, footwork, and facial expressions, making him a revered teacher and performer in the Odissi world.

Odissi dance is a classical treasure of Odisha that combines grace, devotion, and storytelling in every movement. The contributions of the Mahan Gurus have been instrumental in shaping its legacy and ensuring that this traditional art form continues to thrive. Through the tireless efforts of these maestros, Odissi has not only remained relevant but has flourished, gaining recognition on international platforms and attracting a global audience. As a living tradition, Odissi continues to inspire dancers, educators, and art lovers around the world, preserving the rich cultural heritage of Odisha for future generations.

Goti Pua Dance: The Living Tradition of Odisha's Cultural Heritage

Odisha, renowned for its rich cultural heritage, is home to various classical and folk art forms, each with a distinct style and historical significance. One of the most fascinating and enduring of these traditions is Goti Pua, a dance form native to Odisha, especially the Puri district. Known as the precursor to the popular classical dance of Odissi, Goti Pua holds a unique place in the cultural landscape of the region, blending devotion, storytelling, and striking physicality.

Origins and History

Goti Pua, meaning "single boy," originated in the 16th century. During that period, the practice of female temple dancers, known as Maharis, who performed in honor of Lord Jagannath, began to decline. Societal changes and religious reforms contributed to a decrease in women's participation in temple dance rituals. To preserve this sacred tradition, young boys, often between the ages of 6 and 14, were trained to perform in the place of the Maharis. These boys, known as Goti Pua dancers, were trained extensively

to embody feminine grace and poise while performing complex, devotional dances.

Over time, Goti Pua evolved into a distinct performance art. Although primarily performed in temples initially, it gradually became a feature of Odisha's cultural festivals, especially during the celebrations of Lord Jagannath. Today, Goti Pua remains a symbol of Odia heritage, respected for its cultural value and intricate technique.

The Dance Style and Performance

What sets Goti Pua apart is its blend of artistry and athleticism. This dance form is known for its acrobatic movements, intricate footwork, and expressive storytelling. Dancers are trained in fluid postures and complex acrobatic formations that require strength, balance, and flexibility. They often perform stunts such as forming human pyramids, which showcase their physical prowess and are inspired by the devotion of the dancers to their deity.

A typical Goti Pua performance is a visual spectacle of colorful costumes, elaborate makeup, and intricate jewelry. Though the dancers are boys, they dress in vibrant feminine attire, enhancing the dance's visual and dramatic appeal. Traditional Odissi music, comprising mardala (drum), manjira (cymbals), and other classical instruments, accompanies their performances. The songs, often sung in Odia, narrate stories from Hindu mythology, focusing on themes of devotion, heroism, and divine love.

Training and Discipline

Goti Pua dancers begin training at an early age, usually under the guidance of a guru in a traditional Akhada (dance school). This rigorous training includes not only dance and acrobatics but also vocal training, as many

Goti Pua performances involve singing alongside dancing. This holistic approach enables the dancers to connect more deeply with the themes of devotion and spirituality expressed in their art.

Their training emphasizes discipline and physical fitness, with exercises designed to enhance flexibility and strength. The boys learn complex footwork patterns, hand gestures (known as mudras), facial expressions (abhinaya), and, most importantly, the graceful yet powerful movements that are key to Goti Pua.

Cultural Significance and Influence on Odissi

Goti Pua has greatly influenced the development of Odissi, one of India's eight classical dance forms. Several postures and gestures seen in Odissi dance can trace their origins back to Goti Pua. The acrobatic elements of Goti Pua, however, are unique to the style and reflect the young dancers' vitality and agility.

Additionally, the Goti Pua tradition exemplifies the Odia community's dedication to preserving its heritage. This dance is not merely a form of entertainment but a devotional act, honoring Lord Jagannath and upholding spiritual values.

The Future of Goti Pua

In recent years, efforts have been made to revive and promote Goti Pua on national and international stages. Various cultural organizations and festivals now feature Goti Pua performances, helping the art form reach a broader audience and raise awareness of Odisha's rich heritage. Additionally, institutions such as the Odissi Research Centre are actively involved in preserving and documenting the nuances of this art form.

However, Goti Pua faces challenges, including limited funding and a decline in the number of young boys willing to train as dancers. In a rapidly modernizing world, the rigorous training and relatively short performance career (as boys can only dance until they reach adolescence) make it difficult to attract new students. Nonetheless, initiatives by the government, cultural enthusiasts, and local communities continue to keep this art form alive.

The Goti Pua dance form is a testament to Odisha's enduring cultural legacy, beautifully encapsulating the region's devotion, artistry, and resilience. With its rich history, intricate movements, and deep-rooted connection to spirituality, Goti Pua is more than a dance; it is a living tradition that embodies the soul of Odisha. As audiences around the world witness this captivating art form, the essence of Goti Pua continues to inspire appreciation for Odisha's cultural heritage and the timeless beauty of Indian dance.

Embracing Goti Pua, cherishing its origins, and fostering its future are crucial steps in preserving not just a dance but an integral piece of Odisha's identity.

Chhau Dance of Mayurbhanj: Odisha's Martial Dance Tradition

The Chhau dance, an ancient and vibrant dance form, hails from eastern India and holds a special place in the cultural heritage of Odisha, particularly in the Mayurbhanj district. Known for its intense energy, martial elements, and dramatic storytelling, Chhau dance beautifully combines elements of folk, martial arts, and classical dance forms. Recognized by UNESCO as an Intangible Cultural Heritage, Chhau dance showcases the stories of gods, heroes, and demons from Hindu mythology and connects the audience to the ancient tales of valor and devotion.

Origins and Historical Significance-

Chhau dance originated in the eastern Indian states of Odisha, Jharkhand, and West Bengal, with three distinct styles associated with the regions of Seraikella, Purulia, and Mayurbhanj. Among these, Mayurbhanj Chhau stands out due to its unique blend of vigorous choreography and delicate expressions, performed without the use of masks.

Historically, Chhau dance is believed to have developed from martial arts practices, combining war techniques with dance to create a visually captivating

spectacle. In Mayurbhanj, Chhau evolved as a form of entertainment as well as a means to practice self-defense, with its origins dating back to the reign of local rulers. Maharaja Shriram Chandra Bhanjdeo, the king of Mayurbhanj, is credited with formalizing and promoting this art form in the 19th century, helping it become a celebrated cultural identity for the region.

Style and Technique of Mayurbhanj Chhau-

Mayurbhanj Chhau is distinct from the other styles because it is performed without masks, relying heavily on facial expressions and body language to convey emotion. This unique feature makes the Mayurbhanj style more expressive, as dancers use dramatic eye movements and body gestures to portray their characters vividly. The dance form is characterized by powerful footwork, jumps, and complex acrobatic stunts, often performed to depict battles between divine and demonic forces or heroic tales from epics like the Mahabharata and Ramayana.

The movements in Mayurbhanj Chhau are inspired by martial arts and are divided into two categories: Uflis (basic stances) and Topkas (advanced stances). Dancers undergo rigorous training to master these stances, which help them convey the character's strength, valor, and grace. Through rhythmic steps, graceful bends, and well-coordinated hand gestures, they bring mythological stories to life.

Costumes and Music-

Costumes in Mayurbhanj Chhau are elaborate and colorful, reflecting the rich cultural heritage of Odisha. Dancers wear traditional attire with heavy ornaments, often depicting gods, demons, and other mythological figures. Although Mayurbhanj Chhau does not use masks, the dancers' faces are adorned with intricate makeup to enhance their expressions and give them a striking, otherworldly appearance.

The music accompanying Chhau dance is as powerful as the dance itself. Traditional instruments like the dhol (drum), dhamsa, and shehnai (wind instrument) set the rhythm, creating an intense, thrilling atmosphere that elevates the performance. The energetic beats and haunting melodies reflect the highs and lows of the dance, matching the pace of each story and bringing the narrative alive.

Themes and Storytelling

Mayurbhanj Chhau is primarily based on stories from Hindu mythology, particularly focusing on the epics and legends that glorify themes of good versus evil, divine interventions, and heroism. Characters such as Lord Shiva, Durga, and Krishna are often depicted, with battles and divine feats playing central roles in the choreography.

In addition to mythological themes, Mayurbhanj Chhau also incorporates folk tales and local legends. Some performances even depict scenes from everyday rural life, celebrating the beauty and resilience of the Odia people. Through Chhau dance, dancers connect with the audience emotionally, drawing them into an ancient world of mythical grandeur and valor.

Training and Discipline

Training in Mayurbhanj Chhau dance begins at an early age and requires significant discipline and physical endurance. Dancers undergo rigorous training, practicing the specific stances, movements, and postures essential for conveying power and grace. In addition to physical fitness, dancers are trained in facial expressions, as these play a key role in the maskless Mayurbhanj style.

Mastering Chhau also requires knowledge of rhythm and timing, as the dance is intricately tied to the beats of traditional music. Many dancers learn under the guidance of a guru (master) who teaches them not only the technical aspects but also the spiritual essence of the art form.

Cultural Significance and Recognition

Mayurbhanj Chhau is more than a dance; it is a cultural treasure that reflects the spirit, heritage, and devotion of the people of Odisha. This dance form is performed during festivals and celebrations, most notably during the spring festival of Chaitra Parva. This festival, held in honor of Lord Shiva, is a time of reverence and celebration, with Chhau performances being a major attraction for local and visiting audiences alike.

Over the years, efforts have been made to preserve and promote Mayurbhanj Chhau on national and international stages. UNESCO's recognition of Chhau as an Intangible Cultural Heritage in 2010 helped boost its visibility, and various dance troupes now perform Chhau across India and abroad, raising awareness of Odisha's rich cultural legacy.

The Future of Mayurbhanj Chhau

Despite its popularity, Mayurbhanj Chhau faces challenges in the modern era. Urbanization, limited funding, and the influence of contemporary entertainment threaten the preservation of this age-old tradition. However, cultural organizations, local government bodies, and passionate artists continue to work towards reviving and sustaining this unique dance form.

The Mayurbhanj Chhau Academy and similar institutions play a vital role in training new generations of dancers and organizing performances to showcase Chhau on prominent platforms. These initiatives not only preserve the dance but also inspire younger generations to appreciate and connect with their cultural roots.

Mayurbhanj Chhau is a vibrant embodiment of Odisha's cultural soul, weaving tales of bravery, devotion, and mythological grandeur into a mesmerizing dance form. Its martial origins, combined with expressive storytelling and graceful choreography, make it an enduring art form that captures the hearts of audiences worldwide. The preservation and promotion of Mayurbhanj Chhau are crucial for retaining a connection to India's cultural heritage, as it continues to inspire, educate, and enchant new generations.

As Mayurbhanj Chhau graces the stage in India and beyond, it stands as a proud representation of Odisha's artistic and spiritual heritage, reminding us of the timeless beauty and depth of traditional Indian dance.

Danda Nacha: The Sacred Folk Dance of Ganjam, Odisha

Danda Nacha, also known as Danda Yatra or Danda Jatra, is a traditional folk dance and ritualistic performance deeply rooted in the culture of Ganjam district in Odisha. Celebrated as one of the most ancient forms of worship in Odisha, Danda Nacha blends devotion, physical endurance, and community participation. It is a vibrant display of the region's rich heritage and symbolizes penance, purification, and faith in deities, primarily Lord Shiva and Goddess Kali.

Historical Background:-

Danda Nacha has its origins tracing back over a thousand years and is believed to be inspired by ancient Shaivite and Shakti rituals. The term "Danda" refers to the staff or stick symbolizing strength and endurance, while "Nacha" means dance. Traditionally, it is a springtime festival that takes place during Chaitra, the last month of the Odia calendar (March-April). The dance and associated rituals symbolize the defeat of evil forces and the devotion to divine power.

The Significance of Danda Yatra

The festival is observed over 21 days, with each day signifying a deeper form of penance and devotion. During

this period, devotees abstain from personal comforts and pleasures, offering their dedication to Lord Shiva, referred to as Dandeswara or Mahadeva, and sometimes to Goddess Kali. The participants believe that these acts of devotion will bring blessings of health, prosperity, and the protection of their families from evil.

Participants and Rituals:-

The primary participants of Danda Nacha are called Danduas or Bhoktas. They undertake rigorous practices during the Danda Yatra:

1. Preparation and Fasting: Danduas observe fasting, engage in prayer, and undergo strict spiritual and physical discipline. They abstain from comforts and luxuries and often sleep on bare ground.

2. Types of Danda: There are three main types of ritualistic performances:

Pani Danda (Water Danda): Devotees walk on hot sand or through scorching fields to demonstrate their faith.

Dhuli Danda (Sand Danda): Participants lie on hot sand or gravel.

Agni Danda (Fire Danda): Danduas perform near fire, often symbolizing purification.

3. Chaitra Parva and Pala Nrutya: Apart from the Danda performances, Chaitra Parva (festival) and Pala Nrutya (narrative dance) are celebrated, with Danduas narrating mythological tales of divine power, often using the staff as a focal prop.

4. Community Participation: Villagers join in the celebrations, offering food and other forms of support. Community elders bless the Danduas for their sacrifice, and local musicians play traditional instruments, creating an intense atmosphere of spirituality and reverence.

The Dance and Its Elements:-

Danda Nacha involves complex dance routines, often with an element of acrobatics. The dance is accompanied by:

Traditional Drums: Large and small drums set a powerful rhythm, resonating with the energy of the dancers.

Cymbals and Gongs: These instruments accentuate the beats, adding a dramatic effect to the ritual.

Chants and Hymns: Local chants dedicated to Shiva and Kali are sung, enhancing the sacred nature of the event.

The Danduas perform barefoot on surfaces such as hot sand or sharp gravel, displaying their resilience and commitment. They hold sticks (Dandas) as they move in complex patterns, often jumping, rolling, and balancing as part of their routines.

Symbolism and Beliefs:-

Danda Nacha is more than a dance; it's a representation of surrender and devotion to divine forces. The rituals symbolize:

Purification: The rigorous discipline and penance signify purification of the mind, body, and soul.

Victory of Good over Evil: Each ritual act is believed to drive away evil and secure blessings for the entire community.

Unity and Equality: Danda Nacha is a community event that transcends caste, class, and economic divisions, reinforcing a sense of unity and harmony among the villagers.

Cultural Impact and Preservation:-

In Ganjam and surrounding regions, Danda Nacha holds immense cultural value. It has been a source of community pride and a tradition passed down through generations. Although urbanization has changed some of the aspects of rural life, Danda Nacha continues to be celebrated with great enthusiasm.

Many local and state cultural bodies are working to document and preserve this tradition as a symbol of Odisha's folk heritage. Festivals, exhibitions, and tourism initiatives are helping bring attention to Danda Nacha, allowing the younger generation and tourists alike to experience this unique ritual.

Modern-Day Danda Nacha:-

Today, Danda Nacha is also performed at cultural festivals and events beyond Ganjam, gaining national and even international attention. It is featured at cultural events, staged as a performance to showcase Odisha's heritage. However, the original ritualistic essence remains preserved in the villages where it has been practiced traditionally, with the community coming together in devotion and celebration.

Danda Nacha is not just a folk dance; it is a symbol of Odisha's rich cultural fabric, reflecting the people's enduring faith, resilience, and love for tradition. Rooted in spirituality, the festival unites communities, transcends social boundaries, and preserves an ancient way of life. As long as there is devotion and the spirit of penance, Danda Nacha will continue to flourish, connecting generations with the sacred rhythms and enduring power of Odisha's folk culture.

Bagha Nacha: The Vibrant Dance of Ganjam, Odisha

Bagha Nacha, or "Tiger Dance," is a captivating folk dance from the Ganjam district of Odisha, symbolizing the state's rich cultural heritage. This unique dance form draws audiences with its elaborate tiger costumes, dynamic movements, and energetic performances that bring the tiger to life in a vivid, expressive way.

Origins and Cultural Significance -

Bagha Nacha is believed to have originated as a way to depict the strength, agility, and spirit of the tiger, an animal deeply revered in Indian culture. In rural Ganjam, this dance is not just a form of entertainment but also a symbolic ritual. Villagers perform Bagha Nacha during festivals, religious ceremonies, and special occasions, aiming to invoke blessings, protect the community from evil, and celebrate local folklore.

Costumes and Makeup-

One of the most striking elements of Bagha Nacha is the dancers' transformation into tiger-like figures. Performers paint their bodies with bright colors, using black, orange, and white to mimic a tiger's stripes. The makeup artistry takes hours, as each detail is essential to

create a realistic yet theatrical representation. Additionally, the dancers wear tiger masks and sometimes attach bells to their wrists and ankles, enhancing the rhythmic effect of their movements.

Performance Style-

Bagha Nacha combines vigorous, athletic movements with traditional music to portray the tiger's strength and agility. The dancers bend, leap, and crawl, capturing the essence of a tiger stalking through the jungle. Their expressions and gestures convey the fierce and graceful spirit of the tiger, captivating the audience's attention.

Accompanied by drums, cymbals, and other local instruments, the music creates an immersive, high-energy atmosphere. The rhythmic beats sync perfectly with the dancers' steps, amplifying the intensity and bringing a celebratory spirit to the performance.

Social and Religious Relevance:-

This dance form is deeply intertwined with the social and religious fabric of Ganjam. The villagers believe that performing Bagha Nacha appeases local deities and wards off evil spirits. During festivals such as Durga Puja and Dussehra, the dance becomes a highlight, drawing large crowds who come to witness the spectacle. Bagha Nacha not only entertains but also reinforces a sense of unity and pride among the community members.

Preservation and Future of Bagha Nacha :-

While Bagha Nacha remains popular in Ganjam, urbanization and the influence of modern entertainment pose a threat to its continuity. However, local cultural organizations and enthusiasts are making efforts to preserve this art form. By organizing festivals and showcasing Bagha Nacha on larger platforms, they aim to inspire younger generations to appreciate and carry forward this cultural legacy.

Bagha Nacha stands as a testament to Odisha's vibrant folk traditions. Through its fierce movements, detailed costumes, and rhythmic music, Bagha Nacha keeps alive the spirit of Ganjam's rich heritage. Embracing both community spirit and artistic expression, this dance form is more than just a spectacle—it is a symbol of pride, resilience, and the enduring legacy of Odisha's cultural tapestry.

Sambalpuri Dance: The Rhythmic Soul of Sambalpur's Cultural Heritage

Sambalpuri dance, a lively and energetic folk dance, hails from the vibrant Sambalpur region of Odisha. Known for its colorful costumes, rhythmic beats, and joyful energy, Sambalpuri dance beautifully represents the traditions, values, and festive spirit of Western Odisha. Through powerful movements and traditional music, it captures the essence of rural life, reverence for nature, and devotion to deities. Today, Sambalpuri dance is celebrated throughout Odisha and across India as a symbol of cultural pride and resilience.

Origins and Cultural Significance

The roots of Sambalpuri dance are deeply embedded in the folk traditions of the Sambalpur region, where dance and music play an essential role in community life. Originally performed during harvest festivals and religious celebrations, Sambalpuri dance allowed villagers to express their gratitude to nature and celebrate the seasons of life. One of the most significant occasions for this dance is the festival of Nuakhai, a traditional agricultural festival where

communities come together to thank the gods for a good harvest.

The dance has since evolved into a cherished cultural expression that reflects the simplicity, joy, and resilience of the people of Sambalpur. Sambalpuri dance goes beyond entertainment, representing the strong sense of unity and identity of the Odia people, especially those from the western parts of the state. It serves as a bridge between generations, preserving the cultural knowledge and values of ancestors.

Style and Dance Form

Sambalpuri dance is renowned for its dynamic style, high energy, and vibrant movements that embody the free-spirited nature of the region. The dance is characterized by rhythmic footwork, swift hand movements, and expressive gestures that are usually performed in synchronization by groups of dancers. Men and women alike participate, often forming circles or lines, moving in harmony to the pulsating beats of traditional instruments.

One of the distinctive features of Sambalpuri dance is the powerful and lively body movements, which mirror the rhythm of rural life and agricultural activities. Dancers often sway, hop, and twirl with passion, creating an electrifying atmosphere that resonates with the audience. The choreography is simple yet captivating, designed to reflect the everyday lives of the people, as well as their connection to nature and tradition.

Costumes and Attire

The costumes in Sambalpuri dance are as striking as the dance itself. Dancers wear traditional Sambalpuri handloom saris and dhotis, showcasing the renowned

Sambalpuri Ikat, a type of fabric unique to this region. Women typically dress in Sambalpuri sarees with bold colors and intricate patterns, adorned with silver jewelry and bangles that add to the visual appeal of the performance. Men wear colorful dhotis and turbans, giving a rustic yet regal touch to their attire.

The vibrant costumes not only enhance the visual impact but also celebrate the rich handloom heritage of Sambalpur. The dancers' attire reflects the pride the people take in their textile traditions, as Sambalpuri handlooms are famous throughout India for their craftsmanship and vibrant colors.

Music and Instruments

Sambalpuri dance is inseparable from the powerful beats and melodies of traditional Sambalpuri music. The music is typically loud, lively, and rhythmic, created by a combination of folk instruments. Some of the main instruments used in Sambalpuri dance include the dhol (a double-headed drum), nishan (a large kettledrum), tasa (a kind of percussion instrument), and maandal (a type of drum). These instruments produce a resonant and captivating sound that sets the pace for the dance and fills the surroundings with an infectious energy.

The music, along with folk songs sung in the Sambalpuri language, adds depth to the performance. The lyrics of these songs often revolve around themes of nature, love, and devotion, paying homage to gods and goddesses and celebrating the beauty of rural life. The combination of rhythmic drumming and passionate singing elevates the dance, creating an immersive experience that draws audiences into the vibrant world of Sambalpuri culture.

Themes and Symbolism

Sambalpuri dance often explores themes of nature, agriculture, spirituality, and community life. The dance reflects the close relationship between the people and their natural surroundings, with many of the movements symbolizing farming activities such as planting, harvesting, and celebrating a bountiful crop. The dance also includes symbolic gestures of reverence to the gods, particularly during Nuakhai, where the dance becomes an offering to the divine forces.

The themes in Sambalpuri dance highlight the values of gratitude, resilience, and hard work that are deeply ingrained in the culture of the region. The dance is not only a form of expression but also a means to honor the earth and the divine, blending joy with devotion and reflecting the harmonious relationship between humanity and nature.

Popularity and Recognition

In recent years, Sambalpuri dance has gained national and international attention. It is performed at various cultural festivals, competitions, and events, where it continues to captivate audiences with its energy and spirit. Various cultural organizations and institutions have made efforts to preserve and promote Sambalpuri dance, helping to bring it to wider audiences and showcasing it as a symbol of Odisha's cultural richness.

The recognition and popularity of Sambalpuri dance have also contributed to the revival of traditional handlooms, music, and folk art in the region. Today, Sambalpuri dance troupes from Odisha travel across India and beyond, bringing this joyful dance to diverse audiences and fostering appreciation for the cultural heritage of Sambalpur.

Challenges and the Way Forward

Despite its popularity, Sambalpuri dance faces challenges in the modern world, such as competition from contemporary forms of entertainment, migration of younger generations to urban areas, and a lack of institutional support. To sustain this valuable heritage, efforts are needed to train new generations of dancers and musicians, provide platforms for performances, and raise awareness about the importance of cultural preservation.

Government and private cultural organizations, along with dedicated artists and enthusiasts, continue to work toward promoting Sambalpuri dance. Programs, workshops, and festivals are organized to ensure that this beautiful art form thrives and that the younger generations recognize its cultural significance. With continued support, Sambalpuri dance will continue to be an integral part of Odisha's heritage and a cherished symbol of Sambalpur's identity.

Sambalpuri dance is a vibrant celebration of life, nature, and devotion that captures the spirit of the Sambalpur region. With its lively choreography, rich costumes, and traditional music, the dance resonates with audiences by portraying the beauty of rural life and the deep-rooted values of the people of Odisha. As this folk dance graces stages across India and beyond, it serves as a proud emblem of Odisha's cultural wealth and the enduring spirit of its people.

Sambalpuri dance, with its infectious rhythm and colorful heritage, reminds us of the importance of preserving traditional art forms. It bridges generations, bringing to life the stories, values, and spirit of Sambalpur's people, and as we celebrate it, we also celebrate the timeless beauty and diversity of India's cultural tapestry.

Dhemsa Dance: The Tribal Rhythm of Odisha's Koraput Region

Dhemsa dance is a vibrant and rhythmic tribal dance performed by the tribal communities of southern Odisha, especially in the Koraput district. This unique dance form celebrates unity, nature, and the cultural heritage of Odisha's indigenous people. Known for its circular formations and simple yet energetic steps, Dhemsa dance brings communities together to mark harvests, festivals, and joyous occasions, showcasing the traditional lifestyle and harmony within these tribal societies.

Origins and Cultural Significance

Dhemsa dance has its roots among the Gond, Bhumia, and Kondh tribes of Koraput and surrounding areas. This dance is traditionally performed during major festivals like Chait Parab, Magh Parab, and Dasara, as well as during wedding celebrations and other community gatherings. Originally, Dhemsa dance was a form of expression through which the community offered gratitude to the deities for a good harvest or celebrated nature's bounty. The dance is a reflection of the close connection the tribal people maintain with their natural environment and spiritual beliefs.

For these communities, Dhemsa dance is a symbol of unity, joy, and resilience. Through this dance, tribal people celebrate not only their connection to the land but also their strong sense of community and shared identity, preserving their heritage and values across generations.

Dance Formation and Movements

Dhemsa is performed in a circle, with men and women holding hands or interlocking arms as they move rhythmically in sync with one another. The dancers move in a circular formation, stepping forward and backward to the beat of traditional tribal music. The movements are simple but coordinated, relying on unity and rhythm rather than complex choreography. The dancers gradually move around the circle with short, quick steps, often twisting, bending, and lifting their arms, creating a visually captivating sequence.

A unique aspect of Dhemsa dance is that it's entirely inclusive; anyone from the community can join in, and the circle of dancers grows as more people join the performance. As the dancers sway in a rhythmic flow, their movements symbolize unity, equality, and mutual support among community members.

Costumes and Attire

The costumes in Dhemsa dance reflect the simplicity and beauty of tribal life. Female dancers wear traditional sarees, usually made from locally crafted fabrics in vibrant colors, adorned with bead necklaces, bangles, and anklets. The men typically wear dhotis and turbans, adding to the rustic charm of the performance. The attire is often in earthy colors like red, brown, and green, symbolizing a deep connection to nature.

Although the costumes are relatively simple, they are vibrant and stand out against the lush green landscapes where the dance is usually performed. The sound of anklets jingling as the dancers move adds an enchanting rhythm to the performance, enhancing the experience for both dancers and the audience.

Music and Instruments

Music is a vital part of Dhemsa dance, as the dancers move to the beats of traditional tribal instruments. The main instruments used are the dhol (drum), madal (a small drum), and mahuari (a flute-like instrument). The beats produced by these instruments are earthy, resonant, and rhythmic, adding life to the performance.

The musicians often stand at the center or move along with the dancers, creating a close bond between the rhythm and movement. The music is fast-paced and repetitive, maintaining a tempo that keeps the dancers energized and in sync. Songs, which are often chanted in the local tribal dialect, add to the musical layer and cover themes related to nature, harvest, and ancestral blessings.

Themes and Symbolism

Dhemsa dance is primarily a celebration of nature, agriculture, and the community's harmony with the earth. The dance routines depict scenes from everyday life, including farming, harvesting, and community gatherings. The circular formation of the dance symbolizes unity, equality, and the unbroken bond that the tribes share with each other and with nature. As the dancers move in a circle, they metaphorically embrace the cycles of life and nature, expressing their deep respect for the environment and its role in their survival.

The dance also reflects the values of joy, simplicity, and togetherness, allowing dancers to embody the spirit of gratitude and reverence for the land that sustains them. Dhemsa dance, thus, is more than a performance; it's a celebration of life's continuity and the natural rhythms that sustain the tribal communities.

Preservation and Recognition
Dhemsa dance is recognized as one of the unique and treasured folk traditions of Odisha. While it has been performed for centuries in tribal villages, efforts are now being made to preserve and promote it beyond the region. Festivals, cultural programs, and tourism initiatives have helped introduce Dhemsa to a broader audience, allowing people outside of Odisha to experience this beautiful dance form.

Cultural organizations and government bodies in Odisha have taken initiatives to showcase Dhemsa dance at various national and international festivals, aiming to protect this cultural heritage. Such efforts are essential to ensure the younger generations of tribal communities take pride in their heritage and continue the tradition with the same enthusiasm and devotion as their ancestors.

Modern Influence and Adaptation
While Dhemsa remains rooted in its traditional practices, it has also adapted to modern platforms, with tribal groups performing at cultural festivals, college events, and even contemporary stage shows. These performances not only celebrate Odisha's tribal culture but also inspire others to appreciate and preserve indigenous art forms. With modernization affecting many tribal areas, Dhemsa

dance has become a powerful symbol of cultural identity, resilience, and pride for Odisha's tribal people.

Dhemsa dance is a mesmerizing expression of tribal unity, tradition, and nature. With its rhythmic steps, colorful costumes, and infectious energy, it continues to enchant audiences and serve as a reminder of the deep-rooted connection between humanity and the earth. Dhemsa is not merely a dance but a communal activity that brings people together, honoring their shared heritage and the natural world that sustains them.

As this folk dance finds new audiences, Dhemsa remains a proud emblem of Odisha's rich tribal culture, a living testament to the beauty and resilience of indigenous traditions. Celebrating Dhemsa is a celebration of life, unity, and the enduring power of community spirit.

Laudi Khela of Jajpur: A Cultural Gem of Odisha

Laudi Khela, also known as Gauda Nacha, is a traditional and energetic folk dance that holds significant cultural importance in the region of Jajpur, Odisha. This vibrant art form is deeply rooted in the traditions of rural Odisha and showcases the community's devotion, enthusiasm, and cultural heritage. The dance form is characterized by high energy, rhythmic movements, and striking performances with sticks, making it one of the most distinct and powerful expressions of the state's folk culture.

Historical Significance of Laudi Khela in Jajpur

Jajpur, a district rich in history and culture, is known for its vibrant folk traditions. The Laudi Khela of Jajpur is a reflection of the region's deep agricultural and religious roots. Historically, it was performed during religious festivals, especially to mark important occasions like the Dussehra festival and other harvest celebrations. The dance is closely associated with the worship of local deities, and it was performed as an offering or a form of prayer to seek blessings for prosperity and protection from evil forces.

The origins of Laudi Khela in Jajpur can be traced to the rural communities where the dance was an important part of the festive and agricultural cycles. The folk tradition

has been passed down through generations, becoming a symbol of community bonding and religious devotion.

Performance Style and Elements

The performance of Laudi Khela in Jajpur is energetic and visually captivating. The dancers, predominantly men, wear traditional attire that reflects their cultural identity — colorful costumes, turbans, and ornaments. The most striking feature of this dance is the use of large wooden sticks, known as "laudi," which are used by the dancers to strike each other in a rhythmic and synchronized manner. These sticks are not just instruments for rhythm but also symbolic of strength and power.

The dance is typically performed in a circular formation, with dancers moving in harmony to the beat of traditional drums like dhol, nagada, and tassa. The rhythm of the music guides the movements, with dancers displaying both grace and power. They make synchronized turns, leaps, and footwork, creating a dynamic flow of movements that is both athletic and artistic. The tempo often increases during the performance, adding to the intensity and excitement of the dance.

The role of the "Palia" (leader) is crucial in Laudi Khela. The Palia leads the group and sets the pace of the dance, ensuring the rhythm is maintained and guiding the dancers through the intricate steps. The Palia is considered the most skilled dancer and plays an important role in keeping the group's coordination intact.

Cultural and Religious Importance

Laudi Khela is not only a dance; it is an embodiment of the rich cultural traditions of Jajpur. The dance is performed during religious festivals, and its spiritual significance is undeniable. It is seen as a form of prayer, with each movement symbolizing devotion and reverence to the deities. The dance is a way for the community to come together, celebrate their faith, and seek divine blessings for a good harvest, health, and protection from evil.

The dance also plays a role in preserving oral traditions and folklore. Through Laudi Khela, ancient tales of bravery, mythological stories, and moral lessons are passed down from one generation to the next. The community, through these performances, keeps its historical and cultural narratives alive, maintaining a strong sense of identity.

Modern Revival and Popularity

In recent years, there has been a resurgence of interest in Laudi Khela, especially in the urban areas of Odisha. Cultural festivals, both within and outside the state, have provided platforms for this traditional dance to be showcased to a broader audience. Efforts by local cultural organizations and government bodies have helped in the preservation and promotion of Laudi Khela as a vital aspect of Odisha's folk heritage.

In Jajpur, younger generations are taking up Laudi Khela, keeping the tradition alive. Cultural programs, including the Kali Puja and Dussehra celebrations, often feature Laudi Khela performances, attracting both local and tourist audiences. This growing appreciation of the dance form helps to ensure that Laudi Khela continues to thrive, evolving while remaining true to its roots.

Laudi Khela, or Gauda Nacha, in Jajpur is a shining example of Odisha's rich folk traditions and vibrant cultural identity. Through its energetic performances, it not only celebrates the strength and vitality of the community but also serves as a living testament to the state's agricultural roots and religious practices. As the tradition is passed down through generations and finds its place in modern cultural festivals, Laudi Khela will continue to be a cherished cultural heritage of Odisha, reminding us of the powerful connection between art, faith, and community.

Pala Nacha: The Traditional Dance-Drama of Odisha

Pala Nacha is a unique and significant folk art form of Odisha, renowned for its blending of dance, music, and drama to tell captivating stories rooted in mythology, religion, and history. This vibrant performance tradition, originating from the Ganjam district of Odisha, has been an integral part of the state's cultural heritage for centuries.

Origins and Historical Significance

Pala Nacha is believed to have originated in the Ganjam district, one of the coastal regions of Odisha. The art form is closely linked to the religious practices of the local communities, particularly the worship of deities during festivals such as Dussehra and Kartik Purnima. Traditionally, it is performed as a devotional offering, telling the stories of Hindu gods, goddesses, and heroes from epics like the Ramayana, Mahabharata, and various regional myths.

The word "Pala" means a group or a troupe, and "Nacha" refers to dance. Therefore, Pala Nacha involves a group performance that integrates dance with dramatic elements to convey the message of the story being performed. The dance-drama traditionally involves acting out mythological tales, including stories of Lord Shiva, Lord

Vishnu, Durga, Rama, and Krishna, as well as historical or local legends.

Performance Style and Elements

The performances of Pala Nacha are highly ritualistic and theatrical, with the performers donning elaborate costumes and makeup to depict various characters, such as gods, demons, sages, and kings. The actors often wear turbans, traditional dhotis, and ornaments to give them the appearance of warriors or deities.

One of the most striking features of Pala Nacha is the combination of dance, music, and dialogue delivery. The drama is performed in the form of dialogues and songs that are sung in a particular rhythm to describe the scenes and emotions of the characters. The actors take on different roles, enacting the narrative with gestures, dramatic expressions, and body movements. This dance-drama form is mostly performed by male artists, and the performers usually depict both male and female characters in their acts.

The musical aspect of Pala Nacha is equally important. The mridanga (a traditional drum), dhol, tassa, and flute provide the rhythmic accompaniment, with the musicians often participating actively in the performance. The rhythm and pace of the music help to heighten the dramatic tension and add depth to the emotional content of the story.

Cultural and Religious Importance

Pala Nacha is deeply intertwined with the cultural and religious life of Odisha. It is not just a form of entertainment, but also a devotional activity. It serves as a medium for worship and devotion, often performed in temples and during religious festivals to honor the deities. The stories portrayed in Pala Nacha emphasize moral lessons, divine victories over evil, and the triumph of good over sin.

Through its narrative, Pala Nacha plays a significant role in preserving the religious and mythological stories of Odisha, passing them down through generations. The art form is often seen as a way to reinforce community values, cultural identity, and spiritual beliefs.

Structure of a Pala Nacha Performance

A typical Pala Nacha performance involves a narrative structure where the story is introduced, followed by various episodes depicting the life of the central character or deity. The scenes include conflict, resolution, and ultimately, the victory of good. The actors' dialogue delivery is often in the form of rhythmic recitations, which are sung in a way that keeps the audience engaged. The dramatic expressions, such as the mudras (hand gestures) and facial expressions, are crucial for conveying the emotions and themes of the narrative.

The performance is divided into different acts, each featuring a different scene or event. The actors deliver their lines with precision, while the music keeps the rhythm and flow of the performance intact.

Modern-Day Revival and Popularity

While Pala Nacha has been an ancient form of art, it faced challenges in terms of its preservation due to modernization and changing cultural preferences. However, efforts to revive this traditional dance-drama form have been gaining momentum in recent years.

Several cultural festivals and programs, especially in the Ganjam district and other parts of Odisha, have begun to feature Pala Nacha as a way of showcasing Odisha's rich folk heritage. The state government and various cultural organizations have also recognized its importance and are taking steps to promote it.

Young performers are now being trained in Pala Nacha, ensuring that the tradition is carried forward. With its distinct blend of drama, dance, and music, Pala Nacha has also gained recognition at national-level cultural festivals, where it is appreciated for its unique artistic qualities and its deep connection to Odia culture and spirituality.

Pala Nacha stands as a shining example of Odisha's folk tradition, combining the artistic elements of dance, music, and drama into one powerful expression. This traditional performance form continues to be a vital part of the cultural fabric of Odisha, with its emphasis on mythology, spirituality, and moral lessons. Through its revival efforts and cultural recognition, Pala Nacha remains a testament to the enduring power of Odia folk art, preserving the ancient traditions while engaging with modern audiences. The art form continues to foster a sense of identity, community, and devotion among the people of Odisha, making it a cultural gem of the state.

The Juang Dance of Keonjhar: A Vibrant Expression of Tribal Culture and Tradition

The Juang dance is a traditional tribal dance form of the Juang community, primarily found in the Keonjhar district of Odisha. The Juang tribe is one of the oldest tribal groups in the region, known for their rich cultural heritage and unique customs. The dance is an integral part of their religious and social life and is performed on various occasions, including festivals, rituals, and celebrations.

Origins and Significance

The Juang dance is believed to have originated as a form of worship to the deities and spirits of nature. It is performed to appease these spirits and seek their blessings for prosperity, good harvests, and the well-being of the community. The dance form is deeply connected to the animistic beliefs of the Juang tribe, where natural elements like trees, animals, and rivers are revered.

Performance Style

The Juang dance is a group dance, usually performed by both men and women. The dancers wear traditional attire made from locally available materials such as cloth, beads, and feathers. The men's costumes often feature a turban, while the women wear vibrant saris, with distinct patterns and designs that add to the visual appeal of the performance.

The dance is characterized by vigorous, rhythmic movements accompanied by the beat of traditional musical instruments like the dhol (drum), tasa, and flute. The dancers form a circle and perform synchronized movements, sometimes moving in a clockwise or anti-clockwise direction, as they imitate the natural flow of life. The dancers often engage in storytelling through their movements, depicting stories of their ancestors, nature, or historical events.

Ritualistic Role

The Juang dance is not just an art form but also holds a ritualistic role. It is performed during the worship of various gods and spirits, especially during the Chaitra festival (a spring festival) or harvest celebrations. These rituals are aimed at ensuring the fertility of the land and the success of crops. The dance is performed in open spaces, often near sacred groves, to maintain the spiritual connection with nature.

Cultural and Social Importance:

The Juang dance plays an essential role in maintaining the tribe's social fabric. It is a medium for community bonding, where every member, young and old, participates in the festivities. The dance serves as a social event, bringing together families and strengthening intergenerational ties.

In contemporary times, the Juang dance has gained recognition beyond the tribal community, with efforts being made to preserve and promote this cultural treasure. The dance is showcased at various cultural events and festivals, representing the vibrant tribal culture of Odisha.

The Juang dance of Keonjhar is a reflection of the rich cultural traditions of the Juang tribe. It is a vibrant expression of their faith, history, and connection to the natural world. Through its unique performances, the dance continues to play a pivotal role in preserving the cultural heritage of Odisha and offering a glimpse into the life of one of the region's oldest tribal communities.

Dalkhai Dance of Jharsuguda: A Celebratory Tradition of Odisha

The Dalkhai dance is a traditional folk dance from the western region of Odisha, particularly popular in the Jharsuguda district. It is a lively and rhythmic dance that reflects the cultural richness and vibrancy of the region, deeply ingrained in the life and traditions of the local tribal communities. The dance is primarily performed by women and is an essential part of the region's festivals, particularly during the Dussehra and Makar Sankranti festivals, as well as various other celebrations.

Origins and Significance

The Dalkhai dance has its roots in the tribal communities of Jharsuguda, and its origins are closely linked to the worship of Lord Shiva and other deities. It is often performed to mark the arrival of the harvest season, seeking blessings for prosperity and well-being. The dance is also performed during significant social and religious occasions, including weddings and community events, where it serves as both an offering to the gods and a way to strengthen community bonds.

Performance Style

Dalkhai is a vigorous and energetic dance, typically performed by women of all ages. The dancers form a circle or semi-circle and move in unison, gracefully swaying to the beat of traditional music. The performance is characterized by synchronized movements, including hand gestures, leg movements, and rhythmic body motions that depict various aspects of rural life, agriculture, and nature. The dance form is particularly known for its fast-paced footwork and energetic turns.

The musical accompaniment is provided by traditional instruments, including dhol (drum), tasa, mandar, and flute. The beat of these instruments sets the tempo for the dancers, and the tunes often tell stories related to village life, seasonal changes, or mythological themes. The dancers often sing along, adding to the rhythmic energy of the performance.

Costume and Attire

The attire worn during the Dalkhai dance is simple yet vibrant. The women wear traditional sarees, typically in bright colors like red, yellow, and green, along with distinctive jewelry, including necklaces, earrings, and bangles. They also adorn their hair with flowers, giving the dance a festive and cultural appeal. The men, who sometimes participate in the dance, wear dhotis or lungis, paired with turbans and simple jewelry.

Social and Cultural Role

The Dalkhai dance is an important social event in the Jharsuguda region, as it brings together people from different communities, especially during festivals and celebrations. It serves as a way for people to connect with their cultural roots and strengthen social ties. The dance also helps preserve the traditional folk music and rhythms that have been passed down through generations.

In rural Jharsuguda, the Dalkhai dance is performed in open spaces like village squares or near temples, where it often becomes a community affair. As part of the celebrations, people gather to enjoy the music, dance, and festive atmosphere, and it is not uncommon for families to host feasts after the performance.

Contemporary Recognition and Preservation:

In recent years, the Dalkhai dance has gained recognition beyond the borders of Jharsuguda. It has become a significant part of Odisha's cultural identity, being showcased at various cultural festivals and events across the state and even outside Odisha. Efforts are being made to preserve the dance form, and various organizations and cultural groups are working to ensure that it remains a living tradition.

The Dalkhai dance of Jharsuguda is a vibrant celebration of life, culture, and tradition. It not only reflects the spiritual and social values of the region but also serves as a medium for the community to come together, celebrate, and express their cultural pride. As one of the most popular folk dances of Odisha, Dalkhai continues to play a vital role in preserving the region's rich cultural heritage, ensuring its legacy for future generations.

Devdasi Dance of Odisha: A Sacred Tradition of Grace and Devotion

The Devdasi dance is an ancient and sacred dance form associated with the temples of Odisha, particularly within the rich religious and cultural heritage of the state. This dance form was traditionally performed by the Devdasis, women who were dedicated to the service of the temple deities, most notably Lord Jagannath, and other gods and goddesses of the region. Over time, this dance evolved into what is now known as Odissi—one of the classical dance forms of India—although its origins and ritualistic practices trace back to the Devdasi tradition.

Origins and Historical Significance:-

The Devdasi system, prevalent in ancient Odisha, was rooted in the religious practices of the temples, particularly the Jagannath Temple in Puri. The term "Devdasi" is derived from the Sanskrit words 'Deva' meaning god and 'Dasi' meaning servant or maidservant. The Devdasis were women who were dedicated to serving the deity through dance, music, and other rituals. They lived within the temple premises and performed sacred dances to honor the gods, believed to be a form of divine worship.

The Devdasi dance was originally a highly ritualistic dance performed as an offering to the gods, designed to bring prosperity and blessings to the community. The dance was an integral part of religious festivals and temple rituals, with performances held during major celebrations, such as the Rath Yatra and Chandan Yatra in Puri. These dances were deeply spiritual and performed with utmost reverence, often in the inner sanctum of temples or on the temple platforms.

Transition to Classical Odissi:-
Over time, the Devdasi dance evolved, and much of its formal elements contributed to the development of Odissi, the classical dance form of Odisha. The intricate footwork, graceful hand gestures (mudras), and expressive movements seen in Odissi today have their roots in the ancient Devdasi dance tradition. While Odissi has become a formalized and structured classical dance form with specific ragas (melodies) and talas (rhythms), the essence of the Devdasi tradition lives on through this modern classical dance.

However, the term "Devdasi" has a more complex and controversial history. In the 19th and 20th centuries, the practice of temple dancers being dedicated to deities fell into disrepute, as it was misinterpreted and often exploited for non-religious purposes. The sacred nature of their service was overshadowed by social stigma and exploitation, leading to the decline of the Devdasi system. Despite this, the cultural and spiritual aspects of the dance persisted, finding new forms in modern Odissi.

Key Features of the Devdasi Dance:-
The Devdasi dance was known for its graceful

fluidity, intricate footwork, and expressive storytelling. Key elements of this dance form included:

1. Mudras (Hand Gestures): The use of mudras to convey emotions, divine messages, and stories was central to the dance. Each hand movement had symbolic meaning, representing gods, animals, nature, or abstract concepts.

2. Postures and Stances: The dance often involved striking sculptural poses, one of the most famous being the tribhangi (three bends of the body—neck, torso, and knee). These poses were symbolic of the divine beauty of the female form and were meant to evoke the grace and harmony of the gods.

3. Footwork: The rhythmic foot stamping, known as nritta, played an essential role in the dance. The dancers' feet would strike the temple floor in time with the beats, creating an intricate and mesmerizing rhythm.

4. Expressions (Abhinaya): A strong emphasis was placed on facial expressions to convey emotions such as love, devotion, longing, and joy. The expressions, known as abhinaya, helped in storytelling, and were a vital part of the narrative conveyed through the dance.

Ritualistic Role and Spirituality

The Devdasi dance was more than just an artistic expression; it was a form of worship. The dance was seen as a sacred offering to the gods, and the dancers, who were dedicated to the temple, were revered as spiritual servants. The performances were meant to create an atmosphere of divine presence, bringing the gods closer to the devotees.

Devdasis often performed the dance as part of temple rituals, invoking blessings, prosperity, and the fulfillment of vows. The connection between the dancer and the deity

was considered sacred, and the dance itself was believed to be an act of devotion that transcended the physical realm.

Decline and Transformation

As mentioned, the Devdasi system fell into decline in the late 19th and early 20th centuries, primarily due to social reforms and the misinterpretation of the practice. Many temple dancers were forced to abandon their sacred roles, and the dance form itself saw a reduction in prominence. However, some families of Devdasis continued to pass down the tradition, and these practices became a foundation for the formalized Odissi dance that we see today.

Legacy and Contemporary Significance

The Devdasi tradition of Odisha laid the foundation for the classical Odissi dance, which is now recognized as one of the seven classical dance forms of India. Today, Odissi is performed across the world, both as a traditional art form and as a modern interpretation, but its origins in the Devdasi tradition remain an important part of its cultural and spiritual significance.

In modern times, efforts have been made to revitalize the contributions of the Devdasi women to this dance form, acknowledging their roles as pioneers and preserving the spiritual essence of their performances. By continuing to perform and teach Odissi, contemporary dancers honor the legacy of the Devdasi system while adapting the dance to contemporary artistic standards.

The Devdasi dance of Odisha is a timeless tradition that has contributed immensely to the cultural landscape of India. It represents a fusion of spirituality, grace, and storytelling, deeply intertwined with the religious practices of Odisha's temples. While the system of Devdasis has evolved and transformed over time, the core elements of the dance continue to live on through Odissi, enriching the world's artistic heritage. The legacy of the Devdasi dance stands as a testament to the profound connection between art and devotion, reflecting the enduring cultural traditions of Odisha.

Ram Leela of Ganjam District: A Vibrant Celebration of Tradition and Devotion

Ram Leela is a traditional folk performance of the epic Ramayana, primarily performed during the festival of Dussehra. It is a popular cultural event across many regions in India, and the Ram Leela of Ganjam district in Odisha holds a special place due to its unique style and deep cultural roots. The district, rich in folk traditions and rituals, celebrates this performance with great fervor and enthusiasm, marking it as a vibrant expression of devotion, art, and local heritage.

Origins and Cultural Significance

Ram Leela in Ganjam has its roots in the devotion to Lord Rama, one of the most revered deities in Hinduism. The district, situated along the southern coast of Odisha, has a strong religious inclination towards Lord Rama, and the enactment of the Ramayana is not only a theatrical performance but a religious offering. The event typically takes place during the days leading up to Dussehra, which celebrates Lord Rama's victory over the demon king Ravana.

In Ganjam, the Ram Leela is more than just a theatrical

performance—it is a spiritual and community event. The local population, including both performers and spectators, participate with immense enthusiasm, believing that the enactment of Lord Rama's life story brings prosperity, happiness, and divine blessings to the region.

Unique Features of Ram Leela in Ganjam

While Ram Leela performances across India share common themes, the Ram Leela in Ganjam is distinct in several ways:

1. Traditional Folk Style: The Ram Leela of Ganjam has a rich folk flavor. The performances are deeply rooted in local traditions, and the enactment of the Ramayana is often infused with local dialects, music, and folk dances. The language and expressions are in the Odisha dialects of Ganjam, making the performance more relatable to the local audience.

2. Vibrant Costumes and Make-up: The costumes used in the Ganjam Ram Leela are intricately designed, with actors dressing up in traditional attire representing various characters from the Ramayana, such as Lord Rama, Sita, Ravana, Hanuman, and others. The makeup is vibrant and expressive, with heavy use of traditional Odia face painting to depict the different characters in their mythological avatars.

3. Community Participation: One of the most distinctive aspects of Ram Leela in Ganjam is the overwhelming community involvement. The entire village or locality often comes together to perform and celebrate the event, with various people playing different roles. It's not just a professional theatrical performance; it involves families, children, and elders who help in setting up the stage, managing the crowds, and performing the roles.

4. Traditional Music and Dance: The musical component of Ganjam's Ram Leela is primarily based on local folk music, including the use of traditional instruments such as the mardala, dhol, flutes, and tabla. The musical scores and rhythm are designed to accompany the drama and create a spiritually charged atmosphere. The performances often include folk dances that are woven into the narrative of the Ramayana.

5. Processions and Rituals: In many places of Ganjam, the Ram Leela is not just a stage performance but includes processions and rituals that involve the entire community. This could include carrying idols of Lord Rama and other deities through the streets, along with devotional singing and chanting.

6. Sacred Connection to Dussehra: The Ram Leela in Ganjam aligns with the larger Dussehra festival, marking Lord Rama's victory over Ravana. The culmination of the Ram Leela is often tied to the Ravana Dahan (the burning of the effigies of Ravana), which signifies the triumph of good over evil. This public spectacle is a grand finale to the performances, filling the air with religious fervor.

Key Events and Staging

The Ganjam district, particularly towns like Berhampur, Chhatrapur, and others, see large-scale performances during the Dussehra festival. The Ram Leela performances typically span several days, with each day dedicated to specific episodes from the Ramayana. Some of the key events in the Ram Leela of Ganjam include:

1. Sita's Swayamvar: The performance begins with the depiction of Sita's swayamvar, where Lord Rama lifts the mighty bow of Shiva and wins Sita's hand in marriage.

2. Ravana's Abduction of Sita: A significant moment

of the performance is the abduction of Sita by Ravana, which triggers the beginning of Rama's search to rescue her. This part of the Ram Leela is marked by high drama, emotion, and intense performances.

3. Battle Between Rama and Ravana: The final and most dramatic part of the performance is the battle between Lord Rama and Ravana, showcasing Rama's triumph over the demon king. The death of Ravana is depicted through dramatic combat and is followed by the effigy burning in many locations, signifying the end of evil.

Role of Folk Artists and Gurus

The performances of Ram Leela in Ganjam have traditionally been conducted by local folk artists, many of whom have been associated with the art form for generations. These artists are often trained in traditional theatre, dance, and music, and their deep understanding of the cultural context of the Ramayana allows them to bring authenticity to the performance. In addition, local dance gurus and theater experts work to preserve the traditional techniques while ensuring that the performances are engaging and entertaining for the modern audience.

The Ram Leela of Ganjam is not merely a folk performance; it is a celebration of culture, spirituality, and community. It is a time when people come together to relive the story of Lord Rama's heroism and devotion, while also reinforcing the values of righteousness, duty, and good triumphing over evil. The Ram Leela in Ganjam, with its unique folk style, vibrant performances, and community participation, stands as an enduring symbol of Odisha's rich cultural and religious heritage, continuing to captivate audiences year after year.

Ravana Chhaya: The Shadow Play of Odisha

Ravana Chhaya, a unique and ancient shadow puppetry art form, originates from the culturally rich district of Angul in Odisha. This traditional folk dance-drama is not only a reflection of artistic brilliance but also a treasure trove of Odisha's heritage. Its distinct storytelling style and spiritual connection make it a rare gem in the world of performing arts.

The Origin and Significance

Ravana Chhaya derives its name from "Ravana," the antagonist of the epic Ramayana, and "Chhaya," meaning shadow. This art form traces its roots to the Bhata community of Odisha, who have preserved it for generations. The performances are deeply inspired by the Ramayana and revolve around mythological tales, primarily depicting episodes from Lord Rama's life.

This dance-drama serves both as a medium of entertainment and a form of devotion. It is often performed during festivals, especially in temples, to invoke divine blessings.

Artistic Features

Ravana Chhaya is distinguished by its unique method

of storytelling. The puppets, intricately crafted from deer or goat hide, are perforated with delicate patterns to create a stunning play of light and shadow. These puppets, measuring around 18 inches in height, are manipulated against a translucent cloth screen illuminated by an oil lamp.

What sets Ravana Chhaya apart from other forms of shadow puppetry is its lack of vibrant colors or painted backdrops. The performers rely solely on monochromatic shadows to narrate the story, emphasizing the art's simplicity and spiritual depth.

The Performance

The ensemble typically includes a puppeteer who skillfully moves the figures, accompanied by a group of musicians. Traditional Odia musical instruments such as the mardal (a type of drum) and ghungroo (ankle bells) enhance the dramatic effect. The narration is done in poetic verses or prose, sung in the lyrical Daskathia or Prahallada Nataka style.

Current Challenges and Preservation

Despite its cultural significance, Ravana Chhaya faces challenges in the modern era. The art form struggles with a dwindling number of practitioners and a lack of patronage. Efforts are being made by cultural organizations and the government to revive this heritage through workshops, festivals, and academic studies.

Ravana Chhaya is more than just a folk art; it is a reflection of Odisha's profound cultural and spiritual ethos. By preserving and promoting this shadow puppetry, we not only honor our ancestors but also ensure that this remarkable tradition continues to inspire future generations. Angul, the cradle of Ravana Chhaya, stands as a testament to Odisha's artistic legacy, beckoning art lovers to explore and cherish its beauty.

Jamera Ghoda Nacha: The Dance of the Decorated Horse from Bolangir

Jamera Ghoda Nacha, often simply called Ghoda Nacha, is a fascinating folk dance from the Bolangir district of Odisha. Known as the "dance of the decorated horse," it has deep cultural and traditional significance and is closely associated with rituals and celebrations in the region. This unique dance form combines elements of drama, folklore, and music, captivating audiences with its vibrant performances and symbolic motifs.

Origins and Cultural Significance

Ghoda Nacha, meaning "horse dance," finds its roots in the agrarian traditions of Odisha, particularly among the people of Bolangir. Historically, this dance was performed as a tribute to the deities, especially during harvest festivals and weddings, to seek blessings for prosperity, good health, and protection from evil forces. It also plays a role in Odisha's long tradition of animal symbolism, with the horse representing power, nobility, and freedom.

Costume and Props:-

One of the most visually engaging aspects of Jamera

Ghoda Nacha is the elaborate costume worn by the performer, designed to resemble a decorated horse. The dancer, dressed in bright attire, steps into a lightweight frame that is crafted to look like a horse from the waist down. This frame is adorned with vibrant fabrics, mirrors, bells, and colorful decorations that mimic a horse's traditional attire.

The performer holds the reins and moves in rhythm with the music, giving the illusion of a trotting or galloping horse. The costume itself is a marvel of craftsmanship, as artisans in Bolangir dedicate meticulous attention to the details, ensuring that each Ghoda Nacha ensemble is striking and reflective of local aesthetics.

Performance Style and Music

The dance is accompanied by folk music and rhythms produced by traditional Odia instruments like the dhol (a type of drum) and mohuri (a wind instrument). The beats are lively, and the tempo varies to mimic the horse's movement—from a slow trot to a brisk gallop.

The dancer, often a male, performs acrobatic moves, spins, and footwork that convey the strength and agility of a horse. The dance can include storytelling elements, where the performer may enact tales of valor, love, or mythical narratives that are popular in Odisha's folk culture.

Social and Cultural Role:

Jamera Ghoda Nacha is more than just a dance; it is a communal celebration. Villagers gather to watch the performances during local fairs, festivals, and weddings, making it a central part of social life in Bolangir. The performance brings communities together, allowing people to connect over shared heritage and enjoy the artistry that is passed down through generations.

Preservation and Challenges

As with many traditional folk arts, Ghoda Nacha faces challenges due to modernization and shifting cultural preferences. However, local organizations and Odisha's cultural bodies have taken steps to preserve and promote this art form through festivals and performances in urban settings. Efforts are also underway to document the techniques and stories associated with Ghoda Nacha, ensuring that this unique tradition continues to thrive.

Jamera Ghoda Nacha stands as a vibrant reminder of Odisha's folk heritage, echoing the tales, beliefs, and artistic creativity of the people of Bolangir. This dance of the decorated horse captures the essence of Odisha's rural heartland and remains a cherished spectacle, blending culture, dance, and devotion into a performance that delights all who witness it.

Mawla Jhula: The Swing Festival of Bargarh

Mawla Jhula, a traditional folk festival celebrated in Bargarh, Odisha, is a unique cultural event centered around the ritual of swinging, symbolizing the bond between deities and devotees. This celebration, deeply rooted in folklore and spirituality, is a testament to the area's rich cultural heritage and the deep spiritual connection the local community shares with its traditions.

Origins and Cultural Significance

The term Mawla Jhula combines "Mawla" (which is associated with a term of respect or endearment, possibly referring to revered figures or deities) and "Jhula" (meaning swing). This festival is particularly prominent in the agrarian communities of Bargarh, where it serves as a means of seeking blessings for a good harvest, health, and prosperity.

Mawla Jhula is believed to have been inspired by age-old traditions that view the swing as a symbol of joy, love, and connection with nature. This festival provides a way for people to express gratitude and devotion, bringing communities together in celebration and shared beliefs.

Celebration and Rituals:

During Mawla Jhula, large wooden or bamboo swings are erected in village squares and temple grounds. These swings are elaborately decorated with flowers, colorful fabrics, and sometimes symbolic images, creating a festive atmosphere. The central event of the festival involves placing idols of deities or revered figures on these swings, and villagers take turns swinging them gently as a form of devotion and respect.

Devotees sing traditional songs and offer prayers, seeking blessings for peace, prosperity, and happiness. Often, the swings are set up near rivers or fields to symbolize the connection between nature and spirituality, aligning with the agrarian lifestyle of Bargarh's people.

Music and Dance

The festival is marked by traditional Odia folk music, accompanied by local instruments like the dhol and mandal. Devotional songs, many of which are passed down through generations, are sung in praise of the deities. In some instances, villagers perform folk dances around the swing, adding a lively and joyous element to the celebrations.

Social Significance

Mawla Jhula goes beyond religious devotion; it is a cultural gathering that strengthens community bonds. The festival allows villagers to come together, reconnect, and participate in collective joy. The swings become a focal point where elders share stories, and younger generations learn about their heritage and customs.

Preservation Efforts:-

With modernization, festivals like Mawla Jhula

face the risk of fading traditions. Local leaders, cultural organizations, and community members in Bargarh work to preserve this festival, recognizing it as an integral part of their heritage. Efforts include organizing Mawla Jhula events during regional festivals, inviting tourists, and teaching younger generations about the significance of this tradition.

Mawla Jhula is a celebration of faith, community, and heritage in Bargarh. Through the ritual of swinging and the collective devotion of the people, the festival keeps alive the ancient bonds between humanity, nature, and spirituality. Mawla Jhula stands as a reminder of Odisha's cultural diversity, bringing together tradition and community in a joyful expression of gratitude and reverence.

Jhumar Dance: The Folk Rhythms of Balasore

Jhumar is a popular folk dance of Balasore in Odisha, celebrated for its graceful movements, rhythmic beats, and vibrant expressions. Rooted deeply in the local culture, this dance reflects the spirit and lifestyle of the rural communities in Balasore and is traditionally performed during festivals, harvest seasons, and joyous occasions.

Origins and Significance

The term Jhumar signifies joy, festivity, and the gentle swaying movements that characterize the dance. The origins of Jhumar lie in Odisha's agricultural traditions, where villagers performed it to celebrate a bountiful harvest and express gratitude to the divine forces. Over the years, Jhumar has evolved into a popular folk art form, preserving the customs and heritage of Balasore while connecting people with their roots.

Performance Style:

Jhumar is a group dance, typically performed by men and women together, though sometimes separately based on the occasion. The dance features coordinated movements, swaying steps, and circular formations, often symbolizing unity and harmony with nature.

The performers wear traditional costumes, with women dressed in colorful sarees and ornaments, while men don turbans and dhotis. The costumes are often adorned with bells and beads, adding to the visual appeal of the performance.

Music and Instruments:

The Jhumar dance is accompanied by folk music, which includes traditional Odia songs that celebrate life, nature, and folklore. The music is lively, played on indigenous instruments such as the dhol, mandal, and kartal. The beats of the dhol dictate the rhythm of the dance, while other instruments add melody and energy. The music is often improvised, making each performance unique and spontaneous.

Themes and Stories:

While Jhumar primarily celebrates nature and rural life, it also includes storytelling elements. Through the lyrics and expressions, dancers depict themes such as love, valor, mythological tales, and village life. Some performances include humorous or satirical commentary on social issues, making Jhumar not only a form of entertainment but also a platform for social reflection.

Social and Cultural Role:

Jhumar plays a significant role in the social fabric of Balasore. It brings the community together, creating a sense of belonging and mutual respect. The dance is performed during major events, festivals, and fairs, allowing people to come together and celebrate their shared heritage. Jhumar fosters unity and provides an opportunity for the younger generation to connect with the traditions of their ancestors.

Preservation Efforts

As modernization poses challenges to traditional art forms, local organizations and cultural bodies in Balasore work to preserve Jhumar. Efforts include organizing folk dance festivals, workshops, and school programs to teach children about Jhumar's significance and techniques. These efforts aim to ensure that Jhumar remains a vibrant part of Odisha's cultural landscape.

The Jhumar dance of Balasore is a celebration of life, joy, and community. With its enchanting rhythms, graceful movements, and storytelling elements, Jhumar reflects the resilience and beauty of Odisha's folk traditions. By preserving and promoting this dance, the people of Balasore honor their heritage and continue to inspire future generations to appreciate and uphold the cultural richness of Odisha.

Mugala Tamasa: The Satirical Folk Theater of Bhadrak

Mugala Tamasa is a traditional folk theater form from the Bhadrak district of Odisha. Known for its humor, satire, and lively performances, Mugala Tamasa blends drama, music, and social commentary, making it one of Odisha's most cherished art forms. The term Tamasa means "fun" or "entertainment," fitting the nature of these performances that bring together audiences for laughter and reflection.

Origins and Cultural Importance:

Mugala Tamasa has its roots in the rural communities of Bhadrak and surrounding regions. It emerged as a form of village entertainment, often performed during festivals, fairs, and special gatherings. Initially, Mugala Tamasa aimed to entertain villagers while subtly conveying social messages, thus acting as both entertainment and a means of social critique.

This folk theater reflects the values, beliefs, and concerns of the local people. It often addresses themes related to everyday life, relationships, and the human experience, making it highly relatable and popular among the masses.

Performance Style:

Mugala Tamasa is traditionally performed in an open area or village square, with minimal props and a simple setup. The actors, often male, play various roles, sometimes even dressing up as female characters to add to the humor. The performances are characterized by exaggerated gestures, comedic timing, and expressive facial expressions, enhancing the satirical nature of the play.

The dialogues are typically spontaneous, allowing the actors to improvise and add a unique flair to each performance. The humorous banter and witty exchanges between characters are key elements that make Mugala Tamasa engaging and memorable for the audience.

Themes and Satire:

The themes in Mugala Tamasa are diverse, often focusing on social issues, politics, family dynamics, and relationships. Through satire and comedy, the performers address serious topics such as corruption, poverty, and social inequality, making these issues accessible and relatable to the local audience. The humorous approach allows villagers to reflect on these matters without the heaviness that often accompanies such discussions.

One unique aspect of Mugala Tamasa is its use of Mugala—a comical central character who represents the average villager. The Mugala is often depicted as simple-minded, naive, or humorous, allowing the audience to laugh at the character's antics while seeing a bit of themselves in him.

Music and Dance:

Music and rhythmic elements are crucial to Mugala Tamasa. Traditional instruments like the dhol, mridanga, and mandal accompany the performance, enhancing the mood and energy. Dance sequences are often woven into the play, where actors break into spontaneous movements, adding to the light-hearted nature of the performance.

The music sets the tone for different scenes, whether lighthearted or dramatic, and creates a vibrant atmosphere that draws the audience into the story.

Social and Cultural Impact:

Mugala Tamasa is not just a form of entertainment but a social equalizer. It provides a platform where people from various backgrounds come together, laugh, and reflect on the community's shared concerns. The satirical format fosters a sense of unity and cultural pride among the people of Bhadrak, as it brings to light local traditions, dialects, and humor.

Preservation and Challenges:
With the advent of modern entertainment, traditional folk arts like Mugala Tamasa face the threat of decline. However, local organizations and cultural enthusiasts in Bhadrak are working to preserve this folk theater form. Efforts include holding performances at regional festivals, promoting Mugala Tamasa in schools, and documenting its history and techniques.

Mugala Tamasa is a vibrant expression of Odisha's folk culture, blending humor, satire, and social insight in an accessible, engaging form. Through its comical approach to serious themes, it captures the essence of village life in Bhadrak and offers audiences a mirror to reflect on their society. Mugala Tamasa continues to be a beloved art form, preserving the rich cultural tapestry of Odisha while connecting communities through shared laughter and wisdom.

Ghanta Patua: The Traditional Storytelling Art of Cuttack

Ghanta Patua is a unique and ancient folk art form from Cuttack, Odisha, that combines storytelling with musical performance. Known for its distinctive use of brass bells (called "ghanta") and its rich tradition of visual art and narration, Ghanta Patua is a form of "Patua" painting and performance that has been passed down through generations in Odisha. This art form offers a glimpse into the spiritual and cultural ethos of the region, captivating audiences with its blend of visual spectacle, music, and narrative.

Origins and Significance:

Ghanta Patua is deeply rooted in the traditional storytelling practices of Odisha. The term Patua refers to a style of painting on cloth or scrolls, while Ghanta refers to the use of bells. In this tradition, artists, known as Patuas, craft large, colorful paintings that depict religious themes, mythological stories, and scenes from local folklore. These paintings are then used as visual aids during performances, where the artist narrates a story, often involving divine intervention, moral lessons, or cultural tales.

Ghanta Patua is primarily practiced in the Cuttack region, and like many folk arts, it serves both as entertainment and a medium of social commentary. It is often performed during religious festivals, fairs, and social gatherings.

The Art of Ghanta Patua:

The unique feature of Ghanta Patua lies in its fusion of visual art and musical performance. The artist begins by unfolding a scroll painted with vibrant colors and intricate details. The paintings typically feature depictions of gods and goddesses, saints, mythological characters, and stories from the Ramayana, Mahabharata, and other Hindu epics. The use of bright colors, geometric patterns, and intricate detailing adds to the visual appeal of the artwork.

The performer, while displaying the painted scrolls, narrates the story in a rhythmic, melodious style. What sets Ghanta Patua apart is the use of small brass bells, which are shaken rhythmically to complement the narration. The sound of the bells enhances the atmosphere of the performance, adding a mystical and rhythmic quality to the storytelling.

Musical Accompaniment:

Music plays a central role in Ghanta Patua. The artists usually play traditional instruments like the dhol, mardal, and kartal, providing a rhythmic base to the performance. The sound of the ghanta (bells) becomes the signature feature of the performance, marking key moments in the story. The combination of music, narration, and visual art creates a compelling performance that captivates the audience, making the ancient stories feel alive and immediate.

The songs and narratives often include moral teachings, philosophical reflections, and devotional hymns, allowing the audience to not only enjoy the performance but also reflect on its deeper meanings.

Themes and Stories:

The stories told through Ghanta Patua are primarily rooted in Hindu mythology, with a particular focus on the epics Ramayana and Mahabharata. Themes of good versus evil, the triumph of virtue, and divine justice are central to these performances. However, local legends and folklore are also commonly depicted, giving each performance a regional flavor.

The narrator typically uses the visual aids provided by the scroll paintings to help the audience follow the progression of the story. The vibrant imagery on the scrolls adds a dynamic element to the storytelling, while the ghanta bells punctuate moments of tension or climax in the tale.

Cultural Role and Preservation:

Ghanta Patua has historically been a popular form of street theater, where performers would travel from village to village, sharing stories with local communities. This tradition served as a form of education, entertainment, and spiritual guidance, particularly for rural audiences who may not have had access to other forms of media.

In the modern era, however, Ghanta Patua faces challenges. With the rise of mass media and changing tastes, this traditional art form has seen a decline in practice and patronage. Nevertheless, efforts are being made to preserve and promote Ghanta Patua. Cultural organizations in Odisha have started documenting the art form and organizing performances at festivals, where younger generations can learn about and experience it.

Ghanta Patua is a vibrant and unique form of storytelling that showcases the rich cultural heritage of Cuttack and Odisha. Through its intricate paintings, rhythmic bell sounds, and melodic narration, Ghanta Patua continues to offer a glimpse into the spiritual and artistic traditions of Odisha. As efforts to preserve this folk art continue, Ghanta Patua remains an important piece of the region's cultural identity, keeping alive the traditions of storytelling and visual art for future generations.

Prahalad Natak: The Spiritual Folk Drama of Ganjam

Prahalad Natak is a renowned folk theater form from the Ganjam district of Odisha, telling the legendary tale of devotion and divine intervention. Named after Prahalad, the ardent devotee of Lord Vishnu from Hindu mythology, this traditional drama captures the powerful story of faith triumphing over evil. Known for its energetic performances, vibrant costumes, and devotional themes, Prahalad Natak is a cherished art form that reflects the cultural richness of Ganjam.

Origins and Significance

Prahalad Natak finds its origins in the ancient Bhakti traditions of Odisha, which emphasize deep devotion to God. The story is rooted in the myth of Prahalad, the young son of the demon king Hiranyakashipu, who staunchly opposed his father's atheistic ways and remained devoted to Lord Vishnu. Hiranyakashipu tries to kill Prahalad multiple times, only for Lord Vishnu to ultimately intervene and save him, appearing in the form of Narasimha (half-man, half-lion) to vanquish the demon king.

This drama has been performed in Ganjam for over a century and is particularly popular during religious festivals like Holi, Maha Shivaratri, and Dussehra. Prahalad Natak is more than a story; it's a symbol of the victory of faith over tyranny and the power of divine protection, making it deeply significant for the people of Odisha.

Performance Style

Prahalad Natak is known for its dramatic and musical style. It is typically performed on an open stage, with villagers gathering to witness the spectacle. The actors are often male, with elaborate costumes that depict mythological characters like Prahalad, Hiranyakashipu, and Lord Narasimha. The drama involves powerful dialogues, intense gestures, and elaborate expressions, which add to the intensity and emotional depth of the story.

One unique feature of Prahalad Natak is its distinct use of high-energy choreography and stylized movements, making it feel like both a dance and a play. The actors use bold gestures and vigorous body language to convey the emotional and spiritual aspects of the story.

Music and Instruments

The musical component of Prahalad Natak is essential, creating an atmosphere that is both devotional and dramatic. The play is accompanied by traditional Odia instruments like the dhol (drum), mridanga, jhanj (cymbals), and harmonium. The music sets the mood, creating tension during climactic scenes and adding a spiritual ambiance during devotional moments.

The performers often sing verses that recount the dialogues and inner thoughts of characters, adding to the emotional depth of the performance. Songs are sung in Odia and are sometimes improvised, allowing the actors to connect with the audience through local language and references.

Themes and Symbolism

At its core, Prahalad Natak celebrates the themes of faith, devotion, and divine justice. It tells the story of how unwavering belief in God can overcome the forces of darkness and evil. The play contrasts Prahalad's innocence and faith with Hiranyakashipu's arrogance and hatred, offering moral lessons on the importance of devotion and humility.

The appearance of Narasimha at the climax of the play is highly symbolic, representing divine intervention when hope seems lost. This moment is often portrayed with great intensity, emphasizing the miraculous power of the divine.

Cultural Role and Community Involvement

Prahalad Natak holds a special place in the cultural life of Ganjam, bringing communities together and reinforcing shared values. It is a communal event, with people of all ages gathering to watch and participate in the festivities. Many villagers are involved in the preparation, including costume-making, set design, and music.

The performance often extends late into the night, with families staying to watch, sing, and celebrate together. Through Prahalad Natak, villagers preserve their folklore, stories, and traditions, passing them down to younger generations.

Preservation Efforts

While Prahalad Natak remains popular in Ganjam, it faces challenges due to changing entertainment trends and the influence of modern media. Local cultural organizations are working to preserve this art form by documenting performances, training younger artists, and hosting events that promote traditional theater. Efforts are also made to organize Prahalad Natak performances in urban settings, allowing more people to experience this rich folk drama.

Prahalad Natak of Ganjam is a vibrant folk drama that captures the essence of devotion, resilience, and divine justice. Through its powerful storytelling, dynamic music, and expressive performances, Prahalad Natak continues to be a source of cultural pride and spiritual inspiration in Odisha. As a cherished piece of Odisha's cultural heritage, it keeps the legacy of traditional folk theater alive, enriching the community with values that transcend generations.

Paika Akhada: The Martial Dance Tradition of Gajapati

Paika Akhada is a traditional martial dance form originating from the Gajapati district in Odisha, India. This ancient art is not just a dance but a martial exercise rooted in the warrior traditions of the region. The term Paika translates to "warrior," and Akhada means "arena" or "gymnasium," symbolizing a place of physical training and skill development. Paika Akhada combines combat techniques, rhythmic movements, and symbolic rituals, making it a unique cultural performance that celebrates valor and physical prowess.

Historical Significance and Origins:

The origins of Paika Akhada date back to Odisha's medieval period, when Paikas (warrior clans) served as the king's militia. The Paikas were not only skilled fighters but also played a vital role in defending the kingdom, especially under the Gajapati rulers of Odisha. The tradition of Paika Akhada was developed to train these warriors in combat skills and physical fitness, preparing them for battle.

Over time, Paika Akhada evolved from a purely martial discipline into a cultural performance, especially after the decline of the royal kingdoms. Today, it is performed as a folk dance that symbolizes bravery and

the warrior spirit of Odisha. Paika Akhada is particularly important to the people of Gajapati, where it is practiced with pride as a reminder of their rich warrior heritage.

Performance Style and Techniques:

Paika Akhada is characterized by vigorous, rhythmic movements that resemble both dance and combat exercises. The performers are usually male, dressed in traditional warrior attire, which includes dhotis, turbans, and sometimes chest armor or symbolic weapons. The movements involve precise steps, jumps, and acrobatics that require strength, agility, and coordination.

The performance often begins with a ritualistic sequence, where the performers salute the audience or a symbolic deity, honoring their warrior ancestors. They then showcase various martial techniques, including mock battles, weapon handling, and coordinated attacks and defenses. The dance is highly energetic, with performers moving in synchronization, wielding swords, spears, and shields, while engaging in choreographed combat sequences.

The techniques in Paika Akhada are designed to demonstrate strength, balance, and control. The movements, while appearing aggressive, are carefully controlled, reflecting discipline and respect for the martial traditions.

Music and Instruments:

The musical accompaniment in Paika Akhada is essential to setting the pace and mood of the performance. Traditional instruments like the dhol (drum), mardal (percussion instrument), and nagara (kettledrum) create powerful, rhythmic beats that drive the performance. The music is often fast-paced, reflecting the energy and intensity of the warrior dance.

The sound of the drums, combined with the chants of the performers, adds to the drama and excitement of the performance. The rhythm is key to maintaining synchronization among the dancers, and it enhances the martial essence of the Akhada.

Cultural and Symbolic Meaning:

Paika Akhada is not merely a performance but a form of homage to the warrior heritage of Odisha. It is a celebration of bravery, discipline, and loyalty to one's community and culture. The dance symbolizes the readiness of the Paika warriors to defend their people, drawing on the traditional values of courage, resilience, and self-sacrifice.

Each movement and gesture in Paika Akhada has symbolic meaning, reflecting the warrior's dedication to their land, duty, and ancestors. For the people of Gajapati, Paika Akhada is a source of cultural pride, reminding them of their connection to the past and the strength of their heritage.

Social and Cultural Role:

In Gajapati, Paika Akhada serves as both a cultural performance and a social institution. It is often performed during festivals, weddings, and local gatherings, where it becomes a focal point for community celebration. The Akhada not only entertains but also educates the youth, encouraging them to learn about their cultural roots and develop physical discipline.

Traditionally, young men from the community are trained in Paika Akhada from an early age, learning the values of teamwork, respect, and martial discipline. The training in Paika Akhada contributes to their overall physical fitness and mental strength, making it an integral part of community life.

Preservation and Challenges:

Despite its cultural importance, Paika Akhada faces challenges in modern times. With fewer young people learning traditional arts, there is a risk of this martial dance form fading away. However, cultural organizations in Odisha are making efforts to preserve Paika Akhada by conducting workshops, organizing performances, and raising awareness about its heritage value.

In recent years, Paika Akhada has gained recognition beyond Odisha, thanks to cultural festivals and initiatives aimed at promoting India's traditional art forms. This increased visibility has inspired a renewed interest in Paika Akhada, encouraging both the local community and outsiders to appreciate its historical and cultural significance.

Paika Akhada of Gajapati is more than just a martial dance; it is a tribute to the warrior spirit of Odisha. Through its powerful movements, synchronized combat sequences, and vibrant rhythms, Paika Akhada keeps alive the memory of Odisha's brave warriors and their dedication to their land and community. As it continues to be performed and celebrated, Paika Akhada serves as a proud reminder of the resilience, discipline, and cultural pride that define the people of Odisha.

Jhipa Nacha: The Ritualistic Dance of Jajpur

Jhipa Nacha is a traditional folk dance from Jajpur, Odisha, deeply connected to the rituals and spiritual practices of the region. This unique dance form is typically performed during religious festivals and special ceremonies, where it serves as an offering to local deities. Known for its intense energy, rhythm, and spiritual fervor, Jhipa Nacha embodies the devotion of the local people and showcases the cultural heritage of Jajpur.

Origins and Cultural Significance:

Jhipa Nacha has ancient roots in the cultural and religious practices of Odisha, particularly in the temples and villages of Jajpur. This dance is performed as an act of devotion and is often associated with festivals that honor local deities. Jhipa Nacha is believed to invoke blessings and ward off evil forces, symbolizing the community's reverence for divine protection and spiritual well-being.

Jajpur, known for its temples and historical sites, holds a rich cultural legacy, and Jhipa Nacha reflects the region's deep connection to spirituality. The dance is a way for people to express their gratitude and connect with their gods, and it often acts as a communal ritual that binds the community together.

Performance Style:

Jhipa Nacha is characterized by energetic, rhythmic movements that create an intense, hypnotic atmosphere. The performers, usually male, dress in traditional attire and adorn themselves with vibrant costumes, often reflecting the colors and symbols of the deity being honored. Their attire can include bright turbans, long robes, and sometimes body paint, adding to the visual appeal of the dance.

The dance involves vigorous steps, spinning movements, and dynamic gestures that reflect both reverence and intensity. The dancers perform in a circular formation, symbolizing unity and the cyclical nature of life and devotion. Movements are often fast-paced, with dancers entering a trance-like state, signifying a deep connection to the spiritual realm.

Music and Instruments:

Music is an essential part of Jhipa Nacha, setting the pace and mood of the performance. Traditional instruments such as the dhol, mridanga (drum), jhanj (cymbals), and shehnai (wind instrument) are used to accompany the dancers. The beats are often fast and rhythmic, creating an exhilarating and devotional atmosphere.

The music builds up in intensity as the dance progresses, driving the dancers into a heightened state of energy. The sound of the drums, combined with chants and sometimes the shouts of the dancers, creates an immersive experience for both the performers and the audience. The musical accompaniment in Jhipa Nacha is designed to enhance the spiritual fervor of the dance, drawing everyone present into a shared experience of devotion.

Themes and Symbolism:

Jhipa Nacha is deeply symbolic, with each movement and ritual element reflecting devotion, surrender, and unity with the divine. The circular formation of the dancers represents the eternal connection between humanity and the divine, while the intense, repetitive movements signify dedication and spiritual discipline.

The dance often embodies themes of protection, blessings, and community harmony. It serves as a ritualistic call for divine grace and symbolizes the triumph of good over evil, as the high energy and vigorous movements are believed to drive away negative energies.

Role in Community Life:

In Jajpur, Jhipa Nacha is more than a dance; it's a cultural and spiritual event that brings communities together. The performance is often held in temple courtyards or village squares, where villagers gather to witness and participate in the celebration. Jhipa Nacha strengthens social bonds and fosters a sense of unity, as the entire community shares in the ritual and its significance.

The dance is usually passed down through generations, with elders teaching the art to younger members of the community, ensuring the continuity of this cultural tradition. Jhipa Nacha also serves as an important reminder of the community's values, reverence for their ancestors, and their shared spiritual heritage.

Preservation Efforts and Challenges:

While Jhipa Nacha remains popular in Jajpur, modern influences and the spread of mainstream entertainment have posed challenges to its survival. Local cultural organizations and devotees have been making efforts to preserve Jhipa Nacha by organizing performances during major festivals and promoting it as a part of Odisha's cultural heritage.

Some schools and cultural festivals now feature Jhipa Nacha, encouraging younger generations to participate and appreciate the dance form. Through these preservation efforts, Jhipa Nacha continues to thrive as a reminder of Jajpur's spiritual and cultural heritage.

Jhipa Nacha of Jajpur is a powerful expression of devotion and community spirit, combining rhythmic dance, intense energy, and deep cultural significance. As a dance that celebrates divine connection and unity, Jhipa Nacha remains a cherished tradition that brings the people of Jajpur together in faith and festivity. It is a testament to the enduring cultural heritage of Odisha, reflecting the region's commitment to preserving its spiritual and artistic traditions.

Bull Dance of Kendrapara: A Unique Folk Art

The Bull Dance of Kendrapara, also known as Baseli Nrutya, is a traditional folk performance unique to the Kendrapara district of Odisha. This vibrant dance form is a blend of entertainment, devotion, and cultural storytelling, revolving around the depiction of bulls as symbolic carriers of divine energy. Celebrated during festivals and special occasions, the bull dance is not only a spectacle of artistic skill but also a deeply rooted cultural practice in the region.

Origins and Cultural Significance:

The Bull Dance is believed to have originated from the agrarian traditions of Odisha, where bulls have long been considered symbols of prosperity and fertility. In rural societies, bulls play an essential role in farming, and they are often associated with Lord Shiva, whose mount is the sacred bull, Nandi. This connection with divinity and daily life makes the bull dance a significant cultural expression in Kendrapara.

The dance is usually performed during festivals such as Pana Sankranti, Ratha Yatra, and other local celebrations. It serves as a tribute to the divine and an expression of gratitude for a good harvest, health, and community well-being.

Performance Style:

The highlight of the bull dance is its lifelike depiction of a bull. Performers wear elaborate costumes resembling a bull, complete with a headgear that mimics the face of the animal. The costume is often brightly colored and intricately designed, capturing the audience's attention. Two performers usually work together — one acts as the front (head and forelegs) and the other as the back (hind legs) of the bull, moving in perfect coordination to bring the "bull" to life.

The performance involves a combination of dance, acrobatics, and mimetic movements that imitate the gait and behavior of a bull. The dancers move rhythmically to the beats of traditional instruments, often engaging the audience with humorous or dramatic acts. The bull may "interact" with the crowd, creating moments of joy and excitement

Music and Instruments:

Traditional music plays a vital role in the bull dance, setting the tempo and enhancing the overall experience. Instruments like the dhol (drum), mridanga, mahuri (a wind instrument), and kartal (cymbals) create lively, rhythmic beats that energize both the performers and the audience. The music is often accompanied by folk songs, which narrate stories or invoke blessings from deities.

Themes and Symbolism:

The bull dance is not merely entertainment; it carries rich symbolic meanings. The bull represents strength, vitality, and divine connection. Through its movements and actions, the dance conveys messages of harmony between humans, animals, and nature. It often includes elements

of storytelling, where the bull interacts with characters or enacts scenes from local folklore or mythology.

In some performances, the bull's antics reflect human traits, such as stubbornness or playfulness, making it a medium for both humor and moral lessons.

Role in Community Life:

In Kendrapara, the bull dance is a vital part of social and cultural life. It brings people together, fostering community spirit and celebrating shared traditions. The dance is often performed in open spaces like village squares or temple courtyards, attracting audiences of all ages.

The preparation and performance involve collective efforts, with artisans creating the costumes, musicians rehearsing the beats, and dancers perfecting their moves. This collaborative aspect strengthens bonds within the community.

Preservation and Challenges:

Like many traditional art forms, the bull dance faces challenges in the modern era, including competition from contemporary entertainment and a decline in local patronage. However, efforts are being made to preserve and promote this unique folk tradition. Cultural festivals, government initiatives, and local organizations have started featuring the bull dance as part of Odisha's heritage.

Workshops and performances in schools and colleges are also being organized to inspire younger generations to learn and carry forward this tradition.

The Bull Dance of Kendrapara is a vibrant and meaningful expression of Odisha's folk culture. With its colorful costumes, rhythmic music, and engaging performances, it captures the essence of rural life and the community's deep connection with nature and spirituality. As efforts to preserve this unique art form continue, the bull dance remains a symbol of Kendrapara's cultural identity and the timeless traditions of Odisha.

Kela Keluni Nata: The Traditional Folk Drama of Khordha

Kela Keluni Nata is a traditional folk theater form that originates from the Khordha district in Odisha, India. This unique art form combines elements of drama, dance, and music, and is deeply embedded in the rural culture of Khordha. It is known for its engaging performances that blend entertainment with spiritual themes, and it has a strong community connection. The term Kela Keluni is derived from the character Keluni, who is central to the narrative and embodies humor, wit, and sometimes even a touch of satire.

Origins and Cultural Significance:
Kela Keluni Nata traces its origins back to the rural communities of Khordha, where it was performed as a part of local religious and cultural festivals. It is a folk art that has evolved over centuries, with performances often centered around village life, social issues, and religious themes. The central figure, Keluni, often represents an ordinary person, sometimes mischievous, who brings a comedic relief while also delivering important moral lessons.

This folk drama is significant for its role in preserving

the local traditions, stories, and social values of the Khordha region. It is often performed during Nuakhai, Rath Yatra, or other seasonal festivals, where it brings together the community for a shared experience of celebration and reflection.

Performance Style and Structure:

Kela Keluni Nata typically follows a dialogue-based performance structure, with the actors engaging in lively exchanges of humor, wit, and sometimes satire. The primary actors are often dressed in traditional costumes, with Keluni depicted as a playful character dressed in simple, humorous attire to convey his role as a common man. The characters typically include a mix of deities, mythological figures, and ordinary villagers, reflecting the interplay of the divine and the mundane in rural life.

The performance begins with an invocation to deities or ancestors, establishing a spiritual tone before the comedic and dramatic elements unfold. The actors use exaggerated gestures, lively expressions, and slapstick humor to engage the audience. The play often includes elements of social commentary, where the characters mock or satire certain aspects of life, politics, or relationships, making it both entertaining and thought-provoking.

Music and Instruments:

The music of Kela Keluni Nata plays a crucial role in setting the rhythm and enhancing the emotional tone of the performance. The dhol, mridanga, jhanj (cymbals), and bheri (drum) are the primary instruments used to accompany the performance. The lively beats complement the energetic actions of the actors, and the music is often interspersed with songs that narrate important parts of the story or express the emotions of the characters.

The songs sung during the performance are often in the Odia language, and they may contain both folk tunes and improvised verses that interact with the audience. The rhythm of the music is designed to evoke a range of emotions, from laughter to reflection, depending on the scene being portrayed.

Themes and Symbolism:

At its core, Kela Keluni Nata deals with themes of morality, societal norms, and the balance between good and evil. While much of the drama involves humor, it also subtly critiques human behavior, politics, and social hierarchies. The character of Keluni often challenges authority figures or provides witty commentary on the flaws and absurdities of society. His interactions with other characters offer moral lessons, typically underscoring the importance of justice, honesty, and respect.

The religious and mythological themes in Kela Keluni Nata are also significant. The performances often invoke deities and recount stories from Hindu mythology, blending entertainment with spiritual reflection. These themes emphasize divine intervention and the moral virtues that should guide human behavior.

Role in Community Life:

Kela Keluni Nata is a communal art form, often performed in village squares, courtyards, and temple grounds. The performances attract local villagers of all ages, creating a sense of unity and shared experience. It is not only a form of entertainment but also a medium for passing down oral traditions and social values from one generation to the next.

The participation of the local community in the performance, whether as actors, musicians, or audience members, is a testament to the collective nature of this art form. The humor and satire present in the drama foster a spirit of camaraderie and provide an opportunity for people to reflect on their lives, values, and society in a lighthearted way.

Preservation and Challenges:

As with many traditional folk art forms, Kela Keluni Nata faces challenges in the modern era. The rise of contemporary entertainment, the influence of mass media, and changing cultural preferences have led to a decline in traditional performance art forms like Kela Keluni Nata. However, efforts are being made by cultural organizations and local communities to preserve and promote this unique folk drama.

Initiatives such as organizing performances during cultural festivals, conducting workshops, and including Kela Keluni Nata in school curriculums are some of the ways through which this tradition is being kept alive. These efforts aim to engage younger generations with this rich cultural heritage and ensure its continuity.

Kela Keluni Nata is a remarkable folk tradition from Khordha, Odisha, that combines humor, drama, and spiritual themes in a vibrant performance. It reflects the cultural richness of rural Odisha, offering a window into the lives, values, and traditions of the community. Despite modern challenges, Kela Keluni Nata continues to thrive as an essential part of Odisha's folk theater heritage, reminding audiences of the power of storytelling, laughter, and social reflection.

Malkangiri Changu Dance: A Vibrant Folk Tradition of Odisha

The Malkangiri Changu Dance is a traditional folk dance form originating from the Malkangiri district in the southern part of Odisha. This dance is closely tied to the tribal culture of the region and is performed during various festivals and religious occasions. Known for its energetic movements and distinct musical accompaniment, the Changu Dance is a celebration of life, nature, and community spirit. The name Changu refers to the changu drum, a prominent instrument that plays a central role in the performance.

Origins and Cultural Significance

The Malkangiri Changu Dance has its roots in the tribal communities of the Malkangiri region. The dance is primarily associated with the rituals and festivals of the indigenous tribes, such as the Khonds, Mundas, and Gonds. It is performed to celebrate harvests, seasonal changes, and religious events, often marking the completion of a particular agricultural cycle. This dance is a means of invoking the blessings of nature and spirits, ensuring prosperity, health, and harmony within the community.

The dance form has a deep spiritual connection, where the performers express gratitude to nature, ancestors, and local deities. It is also an expression of joy and unity, where the entire community comes together to celebrate important events in the agricultural calendar, such as harvest festivals or other local ceremonies.

Performance Style and Structure

The Malkangiri Changu Dance is performed by a group of dancers who typically wear traditional tribal attire, which includes vibrant costumes, headgear made from leaves or feathers, and colorful beads. The dancers often paint their faces and bodies with natural pigments, adding to the tribal and ritualistic look of the performance.

At the heart of the Changu Dance is the changu, a traditional drum that is played by the musicians accompanying the dance. The rhythm of the drum guides the dancers, who perform synchronized movements, swaying and stomping in a circular formation. The steps are simple yet rhythmic, reflecting the connection between the dancers and the earth. The dance involves quick footwork, coordinated movements of the arms, and collective gestures that are meant to symbolize unity, strength, and connection with the divine.

The performance may feature several short episodes, each focusing on different aspects of daily life, nature, or folklore. The dance often includes storytelling, with the dancers portraying various characters from tribal myths and legends, bringing them to life through their gestures and movements.

Music and Instruments:

The most important instrument in the Malkangiri Changu Dance is the changu drum. This drum is usually made from wood and animal skin, and it has a deep, resonant sound that carries over long distances. The changu drum provides the rhythmic backbone of the performance, setting the pace for the dancers. It is often played with great intensity, complementing the high-energy movements of the dance.

In addition to the changu, other percussion instruments like dhol (drum), madal, and dholki (smaller drums) may be used to add layers of rhythm and sound to the performance. These instruments create a vibrant, energetic atmosphere, which is essential to the overall feel of the dance. The music and rhythm are deeply connected, with every beat driving the performers' movements.

The music is often accompanied by chanting or vocal expressions, which may include invocations to the deities or the recitation of tribal songs. These songs often narrate stories of local heroes, gods, or nature spirits, further deepening the cultural and spiritual significance of the dance.

Themes and Symbolism:

The Malkangiri Changu Dance is rich in symbolic meaning, reflecting the life and worldview of the tribal communities. The circular formations of the dancers represent unity and the cyclical nature of life, where seasons, harvests, and spiritual cycles are interlinked. The repetitive rhythms symbolize the heartbeat of nature and the life force that sustains the community.

The dance also portrays the connection between the human and the divine. The movements and gestures of the dancers are often meant to invoke blessings from the gods or nature spirits, ensuring a prosperous harvest and harmony within the tribe. The celebratory nature of the dance reflects the tribe's deep connection with the land, the natural world, and their ancestors.

Role in Community Life:

In Malkangiri, the Changu Dance is more than just a performance; it is an integral part of the community's social and religious life. It serves as a bonding experience for the tribe, with participants from all age groups coming together to perform and celebrate. The dance brings the community closer, reinforcing shared values and traditions.

The Changu Dance is also an educational tool, as it allows younger generations to learn about their culture, history, and spiritual beliefs. The dance is often taught and performed during festivals, weddings, and agricultural events, ensuring the continuity of this vibrant tradition.

Preservation and Challenges:

Like many traditional tribal dances, the Malkangiri Changu Dance faces challenges in the modern world. The younger generation, influenced by urbanization and modern forms of entertainment, is less likely to learn and participate in such traditional practices. As a result, there is a risk of this art form fading away.

However, efforts are being made by cultural organizations and local communities to preserve and promote the Changu Dance. Initiatives such as cultural festivals, workshops, and performances are helping to raise awareness about the dance and its cultural significance. Additionally, efforts to document and teach the dance are ensuring that future generations can continue this important tradition.

The Malkangiri Changu Dance is a vibrant expression of the tribal culture of Odisha, deeply rooted in the spiritual and communal life of the people. Through its energetic rhythms, synchronized movements, and rich symbolism, the dance serves as a powerful celebration of nature, life, and community. As it continues to be performed during festivals and rituals, the Changu Dance remains an enduring symbol of the cultural heritage of Malkangiri and the tribal communities of Odisha.

Koya Dance of Nabarangpur: A Celebratory Folk Tradition of Odisha

The Koya Dance is a traditional tribal dance form originating from the Koya tribe of Nabarangpur district in the southern part of Odisha, India. It is a vibrant and lively folk dance that reflects the cultural richness and spiritual traditions of the Koya community, which resides primarily in the forested and hilly regions of Nabarangpur. The Koya people, like many tribal groups, have a deep connection with nature, and this dance form is an expression of their reverence for the environment, animals, and the divine.

Origins and Cultural Significance

The Koya Dance is an ancient folk tradition that has been passed down through generations in the Koya tribal communities. This dance is an integral part of their social, religious, and cultural life. It is traditionally performed during major festivals, harvest celebrations, and other important community events.

The dance serves not only as a form of entertainment but also as a means of worship, as it is often performed in honor of their local deities, spirits, and ancestors. The Koya tribe believes in animism, and the dance reflects their

connection with nature and the spiritual world. Through the rhythmic movements, the dancers pay homage to the gods, invoking blessings for a good harvest, prosperity, and protection from evil forces.

Performance Style and Structure

The Koya Dance is characterized by its energetic and dynamic movements, which are performed by a group of dancers. The dancers typically form a circle or semi-circle, holding hands and moving in unison. The steps are simple yet rhythmic, involving a combination of jumping, twirling, and coordinated footwork. The dancers move in circular formations, symbolizing unity, continuity, and the cyclical nature of life.

The dance is led by a lead dancer or a group of male dancers who guide the rhythm and pace. The other dancers, typically women and children, follow the lead with graceful movements, adding to the visual harmony of the performance. The dancers often imitate the movements of animals, birds, and natural elements, reflecting the Koya tribe's close relationship with nature.

Music and Instruments

The music that accompanies the Koya Dance plays a crucial role in setting the tone and guiding the dancers' movements. Traditional instruments, especially drums, are used to produce the rhythm that drives the performance. The primary instrument used is the dhol (drum), which is played with great intensity and vigor. The deep, resonant beats of the dhol provide the rhythmic foundation for the dance.

Other instruments like the tamak (a type of drum), flute, and ghungroo (bells) may also be used to enhance the music. The sound of the flute adds a melodious layer to the rhythm, while the ghungroo creates a jingling effect that synchronizes with the dancers' movements. The music is often accompanied by singing, where the performers may chant folk songs, prayers, or invocations to deities and spirits.

Themes and Symbolism

The Koya Dance is rich in symbolic meaning. The movements of the dancers often mimic the actions of animals, such as birds flying or animals running, highlighting the tribe's deep connection with nature. The circular formation of the dancers represents the unity of the community and the cyclical rhythm of life, which is governed by nature's seasons and the agricultural calendar.

The dance is also a symbolic representation of fertility, prosperity, and divine blessings. The performers invoke the gods and spirits of the forest, asking for protection and a bountiful harvest. The Koya tribe believes that their ancestors' spirits guide and protect them, and this belief is woven into the dance's spiritual expressions.

Role in Community Life:

The Koya Dance plays an important role in the social and cultural life of the Koya tribe. It is not only a form of entertainment but also a way of bringing the community together. During festivals and other events, the dance fosters a sense of unity, cooperation, and shared identity among the members of the tribe. It also serves as a bonding activity, with young and old participating together in the celebrations.

Moreover, the dance is an essential part of religious rituals and is performed at the beginning of agricultural seasons, ensuring that the community receives the blessings of the deities for a good harvest. It strengthens the tribe's connection to its traditions, spirituality, and respect for nature.

Preservation and Challenges:
The Koya Dance, like many traditional folk dances, faces challenges in the modern era. The influence of urbanization, changing lifestyles, and the intrusion of modern entertainment have reduced interest in such traditional art forms. Additionally, the younger generation, more inclined toward modern forms of entertainment, is less involved in preserving their indigenous cultural practices.

However, efforts are being made to preserve and promote the Koya Dance. Cultural festivals, local performances, and community-driven initiatives are helping to keep this vibrant tradition alive. Additionally, organizations and government bodies are working toward documenting the dance and encouraging its practice among younger generations.

The Koya Dance of Nabarangpur is a living testament to the rich cultural and spiritual traditions of the Koya tribe. It is a powerful expression of their reverence for nature, divine forces, and the community. Through its rhythmic movements, traditional music, and symbolism, the dance continues to be a vital part of the tribe's heritage. As efforts to preserve and promote the Koya Dance continue, it remains a significant cultural treasure of Odisha, reflecting the deep connection between the tribe, their traditions, and the natural world.

Kaleshi Dance of Nayagarh: A Traditional Folk Dance of Odisha

The Kaleshi Dance is a vibrant and expressive folk dance that originates from Nayagarh district, located in the central part of Odisha. It is performed by the tribal communities in this region, particularly during various festivals, rituals, and special occasions. Known for its energetic movements, colorful costumes, and rhythmic music, the Kaleshi Dance is an integral part of the cultural heritage of Nayagarh and reflects the deep connection of the community to their traditions, nature, and religious beliefs.

Origins and Cultural Significance

The Kaleshi Dance has its roots in the tribal culture of Nayagarh, where it has been performed for generations. The dance is mainly associated with the tribal communities like the Kandhas and Gonds who inhabit the forested areas of the district. These communities celebrate this dance as part of religious festivals, seasonal celebrations, and during rites of passage such as harvest festivals and weddings.

The Kaleshi Dance is not just a form of entertainment but also a religious and spiritual offering. It is performed to seek blessings from deities, invoke protection, and ensure the welfare of the community. The dance honors local gods, nature spirits, and ancestors, reflecting the tribe's animistic beliefs and their deep respect for the natural world.

Performance Style and Structure

The Kaleshi Dance is characterized by its energetic movements and intricate footwork. It is typically performed by a group of dancers who form a circle or semi-circle. The dancers move in synchronization, executing a variety of jumps, twirls, and graceful arm movements. The dance incorporates fast-paced footwork, which creates a visually striking pattern, making it an enthralling performance for the audience.

The dancers wear colorful costumes, often made from traditional fabrics, and adorn themselves with jewelry and headgear. The attire is designed to reflect the vibrancy of the culture and the connection to nature. The movements of the dancers are often imitative of animals, birds, or natural elements, symbolizing the tribe's relationship with the environment.

The performance is guided by the beats of traditional instruments, with the rhythm driving the dancers' movements. The choreography often follows the rhythm of the music, where the tempo increases or decreases to reflect different stages of the performance. The dance is both a communal and individual expression, with dancers of all ages participating.

Music and Instruments

The music accompanying the Kaleshi Dance is one of its most important elements, providing the rhythm and atmosphere for the performance. Traditional percussion instruments are used to create a vibrant and energetic sound. The primary instrument is the dhol (large drum), which is played with intense energy to drive the rhythm of the dance.

Other instruments like the tamak, a type of small drum, and flute are also commonly used to accompany the performance. The sound of the flute adds a melodious layer to the beat of the dhol, enhancing the overall impact of the performance. The music is rhythmic and lively, often accompanied by chanting or vocal songs that invoke blessings from the gods or tell stories related to the community's beliefs and customs.

The combination of drums, flute, and vocal songs creates an immersive experience for both the performers and the audience, reinforcing the connection between the community, the spiritual realm, and the natural world.

Themes and Symbolism:-

The Kaleshi Dance is rich in symbolism, often representing the tribe's connection to the earth, nature, and the divine. The circular formation of the dancers symbolizes unity, togetherness, and the cyclical nature of life. The rapid, rhythmic movements represent the pulse of nature and the ever-changing seasons, signifying the relationship between the community and the environment.

The dance also has themes of fertility, prosperity, and protection. The dancers seek the blessings of local gods and spirits, asking for a bountiful harvest, good health, and the well-being of the community. The energetic movements of the dancers are a way to invoke divine favor and ensure that the gods look after the people and their land.

The costumes and jewelry worn by the dancers further enhance the symbolic significance of the dance. These adornments are often made from natural materials like leaves, beads, and animal products, representing the tribe's close connection to nature and the spiritual world.

Role in Community Life:-

The Kaleshi Dance is more than just a cultural performance—it is a vital part of community life in Nayagarh. It plays a key role in the social and religious events of the region, helping to preserve traditions, pass down cultural knowledge, and strengthen community bonds. The dance is performed during festivals, religious ceremonies, and celebrations such as harvest festivals, marriages, and other important events.

The Kaleshi Dance fosters unity within the community, as it is often performed by people of all ages, from children to elders. The sense of collective participation is central to the dance, as it brings people together to celebrate life, nature, and spirituality.

Preservation and Challenges:-

Like many traditional art forms, the Kaleshi Dance

faces challenges in the modern era. The younger generation, increasingly influenced by urban culture and modern entertainment, is less inclined to participate in traditional dances. This poses a threat to the continuation of such cultural practices.

However, efforts are being made by local cultural organizations and the community to preserve and promote the Kaleshi Dance. These efforts include organizing cultural festivals, workshops, and performances to raise awareness about the importance of the dance in maintaining cultural identity. Involving younger people in learning and performing the dance is crucial to ensuring its future.

The Kaleshi Dance of Nayagarh is a vibrant expression of the tribal culture and spiritual beliefs of the region. Through its rhythmic movements, colorful costumes, and symbolic themes, the dance reflects the deep connection of the community to nature, the divine, and each other. It is a powerful cultural tradition that continues to play a significant role in the social and religious life of Nayagarh, representing the strength, unity, and vitality of the people who perform it. As efforts continue to preserve this tradition, the Kaleshi Dance remains an important part of Odisha's rich folk heritage.

Lariha Dance of Nuapada: A Traditional Folk Dance of Odisha

The Lariha Dance is a traditional folk dance originating from Nuapada district, located in the western part of Odisha. This vibrant and energetic dance form is deeply embedded in the cultural and spiritual practices of the local tribal communities, particularly the Gonds and Kandhas. The Lariha Dance is performed during various festivals, community events, and religious ceremonies, often marking significant moments in the agricultural and cultural calendar.

Origins and Cultural Significance:

The Lariha Dance is an age-old tradition of the tribal people of Nuapada, passed down through generations. The dance is primarily performed to celebrate the harvest, invoke blessings for a good crop, and seek protection from evil forces. It is also a way to honor the local deities and spirits, which are central to the tribe's animistic beliefs.

The dance is an important aspect of the religious and social life of the community. It is performed during annual festivals, particularly those that mark seasonal changes and agricultural milestones. The Lariha Dance is a collective expression of gratitude towards nature and divine entities, ensuring the well-being and prosperity of the community.

Performance Style and Structure:

The Lariha Dance is known for its lively and vigorous movements, which reflect the energetic nature of the people who perform it. The dancers usually form a circle, symbolizing unity and the cyclical nature of life. The dance involves rapid footwork, rhythmic body movements, and synchronized hand gestures. Dancers often move in a coordinated manner, performing intricate steps and patterns that create a captivating visual display.

Men and women participate in the dance, often wearing traditional costumes that reflect the cultural identity of the tribe. The costumes are typically made of natural materials, with colorful fabrics and beads, showcasing the vibrancy of the tribal culture. The dancers may also adorn themselves with jewelry and headgear made from feathers, leaves, and other natural materials, further connecting the performance to the earth and the divine.

The movements of the Lariha Dance often imitate actions from nature, animals, and daily life, such as the movements of birds or the swaying of trees in the wind. These symbolic gestures are meant to demonstrate the deep connection between the tribe and their natural surroundings.

Music and Instruments:

The music that accompanies the Lariha Dance is a crucial element of the performance. Traditional tribal instruments are used to create the rhythm and atmosphere, driving the energy of the dance. The dhol (large drum) is the primary instrument, providing the heartbeat of the dance with its powerful, resonant beats. The rhythmic sound of the dhol synchronizes with the dancers' movements, guiding them through the performance.

Other instruments, such as the tamak (a small drum), flute, and ghungroo (ankle bells), may also be used to enhance the music. The sound of the flute adds a melodic layer to the rhythmic beats, while the ghungroo provides a jingling sound that complements the dancers' movements.

The music is often accompanied by chanting or singing, where the performers may invoke the names of deities or sing folk songs related to the tribe's beliefs, history, and traditions. This combination of music, rhythm, and song creates a spiritually charged atmosphere during the dance.

Themes and Symbolism:

The Lariha Dance is rich in symbolic meaning. The circular formation of the dancers represents unity, community, and the cyclical nature of life. The rapid, coordinated movements reflect the rhythm of nature and the cycle of seasons, which the tribe believes influence their lives and harvests.

The dance also symbolizes the relationship between the tribe and the spiritual world. The performers invoke the blessings of the gods, ancestors, and nature spirits, asking for good health, prosperity, and protection. The movements and music reflect the tribe's respect for nature, the environment, and the divine forces that govern their lives.

The costumes, made from natural materials like leaves, beads, and feathers, reinforce the connection between the people and the earth. These elements symbolize the tribe's deep reverence for nature and the spirits that inhabit it.

Role in Community Life:

The Lariha Dance plays an important role in the social and cultural fabric of Nuapada. It is a communal activity that brings people together, fostering a sense of unity and shared identity. The dance is performed during festivals, weddings, and other important events, strengthening social bonds and reinforcing cultural traditions.

Beyond its social function, the dance also plays a religious role, with the community coming together to perform rituals and seek divine blessings. The Lariha Dance is a celebration of life, nature, and spirituality, reinforcing the tribe's connection to their ancestors, the natural world, and their cultural heritage.

Preservation and Challenges:

Like many traditional folk dances, the Lariha Dance faces challenges in the modern era. The younger generation, influenced by modern entertainment and urbanization, is less likely to participate in such traditional practices. This shift in cultural preferences poses a threat to the continuity of this vibrant tradition.

However, efforts are being made to preserve and promote the Lariha Dance. Cultural organizations, local festivals, and community-based initiatives are working to raise awareness about the dance and ensure that it is passed down to future generations. These efforts are crucial in keeping the tradition alive and ensuring that the Lariha Dance continues to be an integral part of the cultural identity of Nuapada.

The Lariha Dance of Nuapada is a vibrant expression of the cultural, spiritual, and social life of the tribal communities in the region. Through its rhythmic movements, symbolic gestures, and connection to nature, the dance reflects the deep-rooted traditions and beliefs of the people. As an important aspect of their festivals, rituals, and community events, the Lariha Dance plays a central role in maintaining cultural identity and unity. With ongoing efforts to preserve this traditional art form, the Lariha Dance remains an important cultural treasure of Odisha.

Rayagada Lanjia Soura Dance: A Glimpse into Tribal Culture

The Lanjia Soura Dance is a traditional tribal dance form performed by the Lanjia Soura community in the Rayagada district of Odisha. Known for its vibrant energy and unique style, this dance is an essential part of the cultural identity of the community. It showcases their deep connection with nature, spirituality, and their rich folklore.

Cultural Significance: The Lanjia Soura tribe is a primitive tribal group, primarily found in the hilly terrains of Rayagada, Kalahandi, and Koraput districts of Odisha. The tribe is known for its distinct customs, rituals, and vibrant dances. The Lanjia Soura Dance is one of the most famous dances among them, performed during religious and social events like festivals, harvests, and weddings. This dance form is not only a form of entertainment but also a way to convey the tribe's history, legends, and everyday life.

Dance Form and Performance: The dance is typically performed by both men and women, but the men take the lead. The dancers wear traditional attire, with men adorning a distinctive headgear made of peacock feathers, symbolizing strength and grace. The women wear brightly colored sarees, and their attire includes elaborate jewelry, including silver bangles, necklaces, and earrings. The

dance is accompanied by rhythmic beats of drums and other percussion instruments.

The movements of the dance are characterized by slow, deliberate steps that mimic the natural world, such as the movements of animals, birds, and trees. The dancers often perform in circular formations, symbolizing unity and harmony within the tribe. The dance's hypnotic rhythm is designed to transport both dancers and spectators into a trance-like state, fostering a deep connection with the spiritual realm.

Music and Instruments: The music that accompanies the Lanjia Soura Dance is deeply intertwined with the rhythm of nature. The primary instrument used is the Dhol, a large drum that provides the beat for the dance. Other instruments include Nagada (a smaller drum) and the Mahuri (a wind instrument made of bamboo). The music is simple but powerful, often invoking the sounds of nature and the tribe's ancestral traditions.

Occasions for Performance: The Lanjia Soura Dance

is performed during important festivals and ceremonies, particularly during the Dussehra festival and post-harvest celebrations. It is also a part of the tribe's rites of passage, such as marriage ceremonies, where it is believed to bring prosperity and well-being to the community.

Preservation and Modern Recognition: As the Lanjia Soura Dance is passed down through generations, it faces challenges due to modernization and the encroachment of urbanization on tribal life. However, there have been efforts to preserve this cultural gem. The Odisha Tourism Department and various cultural organizations have been working to showcase and promote the dance to a wider audience through cultural festivals and exhibitions.

The dance not only represents the folklore and traditions of the Lanjia Soura tribe but also embodies the resilience of indigenous cultures in the face of modern challenges. Through performances, this tribal dance has gained recognition beyond its native boundaries, becoming an emblem of Odisha's rich cultural diversity.

In conclusion, the Lanjia Soura Dance of Rayagada is not just a dance form but a vibrant expression of the Lanjia Soura tribe's spiritual connection with nature and their rich cultural heritage. Its continued performance and preservation are vital in safeguarding the unique traditions of the tribe for future generations.

Sonepur Mayala Joda: A Unique Tribal Dance of Odisha

Sonepur, a picturesque district in the western part of Odisha, is home to a rich cultural heritage that includes various tribal communities. One of the lesser-known but fascinating cultural traditions of this region is the Mayala Joda, a traditional tribal dance that holds significant cultural importance for the people of Sonepur. The dance is an integral part of the celebrations and rituals of the local tribal communities, often performed during religious festivals and special occasions.

Origin and Cultural Context: The term "Mayala Joda" is derived from two words: "Mayala," which refers to the male and female, and "Joda," meaning pair or couple. The dance is traditionally performed by two individuals – one male and one female – who represent the concept of harmony and unity in life. This dance is rooted in the folklore, agricultural practices, and spirituality of the tribal people of Sonepur.

The dance is primarily associated with the agricultural cycle, especially during harvest festivals. It is performed to celebrate the bounty of nature and to seek blessings

for a prosperous future. The dance is deeply symbolic, expressing the unity of the earth and sky, the male and female energies, and the relationship between humans and nature.

Performance and Dance Style: The Mayala Joda dance is performed by a couple, typically a man and a woman, dressed in traditional attire. The male dancer usually wears a dhoti or lungi, with a simple headgear, while the female dancer wears a saree or traditional costume with bright jewelry and adornments. Both dancers perform synchronized movements that embody grace, energy, and harmony. The dance is often marked by rhythmic steps, circular formations, and symbolic gestures that mimic the flow of nature, such as the wind, rain, or the movement of animals.

The male dancer typically leads the pair, guiding the female dancer through a series of intricate footwork and gestures. The female dancer follows in perfect coordination, representing the balance between the two forces. The dance also incorporates elements of storytelling, where the dancers mime scenes from rural life, agricultural work, or ancient myths and legends.

Music and Instruments: The music that accompanies the Mayala Joda dance is lively and rhythm-driven, played using traditional instruments like the Dhol (drum), Bata (another type of drum), and Mahuri (flute). These instruments help maintain the beat and rhythm of the dance, creating an enchanting atmosphere. The lively beats of the drum create a pulsating energy, while the melody from the Mahuri adds a mystical and spiritual layer to the performance.

Occasions for Performance: Mayala Joda is typically performed during various tribal festivals and community gatherings in Sonepur. These include harvest festivals, religious rituals, and local celebrations such as Nuakhai (a festival marking the first day of the new harvest). The dance is believed to bring good fortune, fertility, and prosperity to the community, making it an essential part of the local cultural practices.

The dance also features prominently in marriages and other important social events within the tribe. During these events, Mayala Joda symbolizes the union of two individuals, just as the dance symbolizes the union of different elements of nature.

Preservation and Recognition: Like many other tribal traditions, the Mayala Joda dance faces the challenge of preservation in the face of modernization. However, local cultural organizations, tribal associations, and the Odisha Tourism Department have made efforts to safeguard and promote this unique art form. Cultural festivals and tribal exhibitions are increasingly being organized, allowing audiences from outside the region to experience this vibrant dance form.

The Mayala Joda dance is a celebration of life, nature, and the unity between human beings and the natural world. Its colorful performances and rhythmic beats embody the spirit of the tribal people of Sonepur, and it continues to be a vital part of the cultural fabric of Odisha. By keeping these traditions alive, the community ensures that future generations remain connected to their heritage and the rich history of the tribal culture in the region.

Domkach of Sundargarh: A Vibrant Tribal Dance of Odisha

The Domkach is a traditional dance form originating from the Sundargarh district of Odisha, predominantly performed by the Munda tribe. This dance is deeply embedded in the tribal culture of the region and is an expression of the community's connection to nature, rituals, and their cultural heritage. The Domkach dance is not just a form of entertainment but is also an important medium for conveying the tribe's stories, beliefs, and rituals.

Cultural Significance:
Sundargarh, a district in western Odisha, is home to various indigenous tribal communities, with the Munda tribe being one of the prominent groups. The Domkach dance holds great cultural and religious significance for the Mundas and is performed during important events like festivals, marriages, harvests, and other community rituals. It is considered a sacred dance, performed to appease the deities, celebrate nature's abundance, and strengthen social bonds within the community.

The dance is often linked to the Sohrai festival, a post-harvest celebration that honors the agricultural cycle and the relationship between the people and the land. It is believed that through the dance, the dancers seek blessings for prosperity, fertility, and protection from evil spirits.

Performance and Dance Style:

The Domkach dance is performed by both men and women of the Munda tribe, and it is characterized by its vibrant, energetic movements. The dance is performed in a circle, symbolizing unity and harmony among the tribe members. The steps are rhythmic, involving swift footwork, high jumps, and intricate body movements that are synchronized with the beat of the drums.

Dancers perform in a disciplined formation, often moving in a circular or semi-circular pattern, with their arms raised or outstretched, signifying a connection with nature and the divine. The movements mimic the natural elements like the flowing of water, the swaying of trees, and the movements of animals. This connection to nature is central to the dance, as the Mundas view the earth as sacred.

Costumes and Attire:

The traditional attire worn by the dancers is simple yet colorful, reflecting the vibrant culture of the Munda tribe. Men typically wear a dhoti or lungi, along with a traditional headgear made of feathers, which symbolizes bravery and strength. Women wear bright sarees or skirts, adorned with traditional jewelry such as earrings, necklaces, and bangles made of metal or beads. The headgear worn by women often features decorative motifs, adding to the dance's visual appeal.

The costumes, combined with the rhythmic movements and energetic performance, create a mesmerizing atmosphere that captivates both dancers and spectators alike.

Music and Instruments:

The music that accompanies the Domkach dance is an essential part of the performance. The primary instrument used in this dance is the Dhol, a large, traditional drum, which provides the rhythmic beat for the dancers. The drumming is often accompanied by other percussion instruments such as the Nagara (another type of drum) and Mahuri (a flute), creating an immersive musical experience.

The beat of the Dhol is fast-paced and lively, driving the dancers' movements. The music's repetitive rhythm is meant to bring the dancers into a trance-like state, heightening the spiritual and ritualistic aspects of the dance.

Occasions for Performance:

The Domkach dance is most commonly performed during the Sohrai festival, marking the end of the harvest season and the beginning of the new agricultural cycle. It is also performed during important community events such as weddings, initiation rites, and rituals to honor deities. The dance serves as a form of thanksgiving for the bountiful harvest and as a prayer for continued prosperity.

In addition to these, the Domkach is also performed during public celebrations, such as community feasts and other social gatherings, further strengthening the bonds within the tribal community.

Preservation and Recognition:
Like many indigenous dance forms, Domkach faces the threat of losing its traditional appeal due to modernization and changing social structures. However, efforts are being made by local cultural organizations, the government, and tourism departments to preserve this vibrant tradition. Cultural festivals and tribal fairs are increasingly being organized to showcase the Domkach dance, allowing it to reach wider audiences and ensuring its survival for future generations.

In recent years, the Domkach dance has also gained recognition at regional and national cultural events, helping raise awareness about the unique tribal cultures of Odisha.

The Domkach dance of Sundargarh is a beautiful, energetic expression of the Munda tribe's deep connection to nature, their spirituality, and their rich cultural heritage. With its rhythmic movements, colorful attire, and spiritual significance, the dance is an important cultural asset of Odisha. As the dance continues to be performed during important community events, it remains a living testament to the tribe's resilience and the vibrancy of Odisha's tribal culture.

Jodi Sankha of Ganjam: A Symbol of Tradition and Devotion

The Jodi Sankha is a traditional ritual performed in the coastal region of Odisha, particularly in the Ganjam district. It involves the blowing of conch shells by a pair, often as part of religious rituals or festivals. The term "Jodi Sankha" means "pair of conch shells," where "Jodi" signifies a pair, and "Sankha" refers to the conch shell. The practice is deeply rooted in the spiritual and cultural traditions of the local people, and it holds significant religious importance, especially in the temples and during major festivals.

Cultural Significance:

The Jodi Sankha ritual has a rich history in Odisha, particularly in the Ganjam region, where conch shells are considered sacred and are believed to possess spiritual powers. The blowing of the conch shells is a way to invoke the presence of deities, purify the surroundings, and create a divine atmosphere during religious ceremonies.

In Hinduism, conch shells are believed to have been used by the gods in ancient times, and they are mentioned in many sacred texts, including the Mahabharata and

the Puranas. The sound of the conch is said to symbolize the cosmic sound or "Om," the eternal vibration of the universe. The act of blowing the Jodi Sankha is seen as a call to the divine, an offering of respect, and an invocation of blessings.

Performance and Rituals:

The Jodi Sankha ritual is often performed during religious festivals, temple rituals, and community celebrations. During these events, a pair of conch shells—often large, beautifully decorated, and considered to be of high spiritual significance—are blown by two individuals. The sound produced by the conch is loud, resonating through the surroundings, and is meant to reach the heavens, carrying prayers and offerings to the gods.

The individuals performing the ritual usually stand facing each other, each holding one of the conch shells. They blow into the shells simultaneously, creating a harmonious, powerful sound that is believed to purify the air and energize the space. The ritual is often performed in temples, particularly during important events such as Rath Yatra, Shivaratri, Durga Puja, and other local festivals.

The blowing of the Jodi Sankha is accompanied by prayers, hymns, and devotional songs. The sound of the conch serves as a prelude to the beginning of the worship, signaling the commencement of sacred rites and rituals.

Symbolism and Spiritual Meaning:

The Jodi Sankha is not just a physical act but is rich in symbolism. The sound of the conch is considered auspicious and is believed to have the power to ward off evil spirits, bring prosperity, and ensure the protection of the devotees. It is also said to signify the arrival of divine energy, creating a connection between the human world and the divine realm.

The conch shells used in the ritual are carefully chosen, as they are believed to possess certain energies. The larger and more beautifully crafted the shell, the greater its spiritual power. The synchronized blowing of the two conch shells symbolizes harmony and balance, and it is also seen as an embodiment of the duality of existence—such as the union of the masculine and feminine energies, the material and the spiritual, or the earth and the heavens.

Occasions for the Jodi Sankha Ritual:

The Jodi Sankha is traditionally performed during significant religious occasions, including:

1. Rath Yatra: The annual festival dedicated to Lord Jagannath, celebrated with much grandeur in Puri, and also in temples in the Ganjam district, often sees the blowing of Jodi Sankha as a part of the religious rites.

2. Durga Puja: The ritual is an important feature during the Durga Puja festivities in Odisha, where the Jodi Sankha is blown to invoke the blessings of Goddess Durga.

3. Shivaratri: On this auspicious night dedicated to Lord Shiva, the Jodi Sankha is blown during the temple rituals as a form of worship and devotion.

4. Local Festivals and Marriages: In Ganjam, Jodi Sankha is also blown during important social and cultural events, such as local fairs, marriages, and community feasts, to mark the beginning of the celebrations.

Preservation and Recognition:

The Jodi Sankha ritual, like many other traditional practices in Odisha, faces the challenge of modernization and the gradual decline of ancient customs. However, efforts are being made to preserve and promote this sacred tradition through cultural programs, temple festivals, and regional celebrations. It is a unique cultural expression of Odisha's devotion to its gods, and its continuation is important for maintaining the region's religious and cultural identity.

In recent years, the Jodi Sankha has gained attention outside of the region, especially during cultural tourism events, showcasing the rich spiritual and cultural practices of the Ganjam district. The practice continues to be a symbol of unity, spirituality, and devotion for the people of Odisha.

The Jodi Sankha of Ganjam is a beautiful and powerful ritual that reflects the deep spiritual traditions of Odisha. Through the blowing of the conch shells, the community calls upon divine blessings, strengthens their faith, and celebrates their connection with the divine forces. This sacred act, performed in pairs, embodies unity, harmony, and reverence, making it an essential part of the religious and cultural fabric of the region. As a vibrant tradition of Ganjam, it continues to inspire devotion and awe, preserving the spiritual essence of Odisha's tribal and cultural heritage.

Maipi Kandana Gita: The Vibrant Folk Dance of Cuttack's Agricultural Heritage

Maipi Kandana Gita is a traditional folk dance from the Cuttack district of Odisha, India. It is an integral part of the cultural heritage of the region and is usually performed during festivals and religious occasions. The dance is closely associated with the agricultural practices and seasonal changes of the area.

In Maipi Kandana Gita, the dancers typically depict the farming activities, which are crucial to the rural lifestyle in Odisha. The performers sing songs (known as Gita) that tell stories related to agriculture, the changing seasons, or deities associated with the land, like Lord Jagannath. The dances usually reflect the emotions of joy, celebration, and sometimes reverence for nature.

The dance is generally characterized by vibrant and energetic movements, and the performers wear traditional attire, often in bright colors. The accompanying music includes local instruments like dhol, mardala, and flutes, creating an atmospheric and lively rhythm that enhances the performance.

This folk dance serves as both a cultural expression and a social gathering, bringing together communities and celebrating the traditions and values of Odisha. The songs performed during Maipi Kandana Gita often serve as a medium to pass down stories and folklore from one generation to the next.

Radha Prem Leela: The Divine Love Play of Ganjam District

Radha Prem Leela is a traditional folk performance that originates from the Ganjam district of southern Odisha, India. This captivating art form is deeply rooted in the region's Vaishnavite culture, primarily revolving around the divine love story of Lord Krishna and Radha. The performances depict the romantic and spiritual bond between Krishna and Radha, emphasizing themes of devotion, love, and divine play.

The name "Radha Prem Leela" translates to "The Divine Love Play of Radha," and the dance-drama form reflects the eternal and pure love that Radha and Krishna shared. It is a celebration of love in its most spiritual and divine form, which has been a significant part of the religious and cultural fabric of Odisha for centuries.

Performance Style:

Radha Prem Leela is usually performed during specific festivals in the Ganjam district, such as Dola Yatra (celebrated on Phalgun Purnima) and Jhulan Yatra (held during the month of Shravan). These festivals are dedicated to Lord Krishna and celebrate his divine leelas (plays) along with the eternal love story of Radha and Krishna.

The performance typically involves a combination

of dance, music, and storytelling, where actors portray different episodes from Krishna's life, especially his playful interactions with Radha. The performances are often staged in open spaces, temples, or community gathering areas, where people from the local community gather to witness the spectacle.

The characters involved in the performances include Krishna, Radha, and other figures from Hindu mythology, with the performers wearing traditional attire, such as colorful costumes and accessories that enhance the divine theme of the play. The performances are deeply devotional and are filled with expressions of love, longing, and spiritual joy.

Musical Accompaniment:

The musical element of Radha Prem Leela is integral to its atmosphere. The performances are typically accompanied by traditional instruments, such as the Dhol, Mahuri, Chagha, and Flute, which are used to create a rhythmic and melodious soundscape that draws the audience deeper into the devotional experience. The music resonates with the themes of the performance, invoking a sense of peace, love, and devotion.

The songs sung during the play often include devotional hymns (bhajans) dedicated to Lord Krishna and Radha, and they play a key role in narrating the storylines. The music enhances the emotional impact of the performance, with the rhythm and melody bringing the divine love story to life.

Cultural Significance:

Radha Prem Leela is not only a form of artistic expression but also holds immense cultural and spiritual significance in the Ganjam district. It serves as a means to impart moral lessons about love, devotion, and the importance of faith in the divine. Through these performances, the local community connects with their cultural roots, and the younger generation is introduced to the teachings of Lord Krishna.

The performance serves as a reflection of the region's deep connection to Hindu mythology, particularly the stories associated with Lord Krishna. It is an important part of the festivals celebrated in Ganjam and other parts of Odisha, keeping the traditions alive and helping to preserve the rich cultural heritage of the region.

Radha Prem Leela continues to be a vibrant and cherished part of Odisha's folk traditions. The performances bring together communities and offer a platform for spiritual and cultural expression. The depiction of Radha and Krishna's love story transcends mere theatrical entertainment, becoming a form of worship, devotion, and community bonding.

For those who wish to experience this powerful and spiritually enriching performance, attending festivals like Dola Yatra or Jhulan Yatra in Ganjam district offers an opportunity to witness the Radha Prem Leela firsthand. Whether through the energetic dance movements or the soulful devotional music, Radha Prem Leela offers a glimpse into the timeless bond of divine love, bringing both devotees and spectators closer to the divine.

Rayagada Paraja Saura Dance: A Vibrant Celebration of Tribal Culture and Devotion

The Paraja Saura Dance is a traditional tribal dance form from the Rayagada district in southern Odisha, primarily performed by the indigenous Paraja and Saura tribes. This dance is an important aspect of the region's rich cultural heritage, showcasing the lifestyle, rituals, and beliefs of these tribal communities. The Paraja and Saura tribes, known for their deep connection to nature and the land, use this dance form to celebrate life, agriculture, and religious beliefs.

Performance Style:
The Paraja Saura Dance is performed during various community festivals, including harvest festivals, weddings, and other cultural gatherings. It is an expression of joy, devotion, and gratitude toward nature and the gods. The dance is characterized by vibrant movements, rhythmic footwork, and energetic patterns that reflect the energy of the performers.

The dancers typically form circles or semi-circles and perform synchronized steps, often imitating the movements of nature, animals, or deities. The dance movements are

symbolic of the agricultural cycle, with dances reflecting the stages of farming, such as planting, growing, and harvesting crops. It is a celebration of the bond between the tribal people and the land they cultivate.

Costumes and Attire:

The attire for the Paraja Saura Dance is colorful and reflective of the tribal community's lifestyle. The performers typically wear traditional tribal dress, which includes simple yet vibrant clothing made from local materials. Men often wear dhotis or lungis, while women wear sarees or skirts. Both men and women wear adornments like necklaces, bangles, and beads, which add to the festive atmosphere of the performance.

Musical Accompaniment:

The Paraja Saura Dance is accompanied by traditional tribal music, played on instruments such as the dhol, mandal, flute, ghanti (bells), and tamak (drums). The beats of these instruments set the rhythm for the dance and enhance the overall experience. The music is lively and rhythmic, with each instrument playing a crucial role in creating an immersive environment for the dance. The music is integral to the performance, guiding the dancers and imbuing the performance with energy and emotion.

Cultural Significance:

The Paraja Saura Dance is not only a cultural performance but also a medium for the community to express their gratitude to nature, the gods, and their ancestors. The dance often represents important themes of fertility, agricultural prosperity, and the cycle of life. It serves as a reminder of the deep connection that these tribes have with their land and environment.

Through this dance, the Paraja and Saura tribes pass down their traditions, folklore, and history from generation to generation. The dance also reinforces the sense of community, as it is typically performed in groups, fostering unity and togetherness.

The Paraja Saura Dance is a beautiful and powerful folk tradition that reflects the cultural richness of the tribal communities in the Rayagada district of Odisha. It is a dance of joy, devotion, and respect for nature, expressing the deep-rooted bond between the people and the land they live on. The vibrant movements, colorful attire, and rhythmic music make this dance a captivating spectacle that continues to be an important part of the tribal identity and cultural heritage of Odisha.

For those seeking an authentic cultural experience, witnessing the Paraja Saura Dance during local festivals in Rayagada offers a unique opportunity to immerse in the traditions and spirit of the tribal communities of Odisha

Chadheya Dance of Ganjam: A Folk Symphony of Love, Nature, and Social Awakening

"Mistakes can be forgiven, but crimes against humanity and nature cannot. Caste is not God-made, but man-made — and humanity should rise above it."

These timeless truths echo powerfully through the traditional folk performance known as Chadheya Dance, an extraordinary cultural gem from the Ganjam district of southern Odisha.

Rooted deeply in tribal customs and rural life, Chadheya Dance is much more than a festive performance — it is a vivid blend of mythological narrative, social commentary, and aesthetic expression. Performed primarily during Danda Nacha, a sacred ritual festival dedicated to Lord Shiva and Goddess Kali, this dance captures the pulse of the land — its love, struggles, faith, and social evolution.

The Myth Behind the Movement: Chadheya and the Divine Test

At the heart of this performance lies a mythological tale that serves as a moral compass for society. Chadheya, a tribal man blessed by Lord Shiva with a divine weapon (passa), becomes the protagonist of a tale that teaches humility and the dangers of misjudgment.

While in the forest, Chadheya witnesses a pair of doves in a moment of intimacy — unaware that they are none other than Lord Shiva and Goddess Parvati in disguise. Failing to recognize their divine presence, Chadheya hurls his weapon at them. Enraged, Lord Shiva punishes him with death by snakebite.

What follows is a profound spiritual and social lesson. Chadheya's two wives, Chadeyanīs, weep and plead for his life. The divine couple reappears — but this time, in the guise of so-called underprivileged castes such as Keuta-Keutani (fisherfolk), Dhiba (washermen), and Dhobuni (laundresses). The community fails to recognize the divine in them, underscoring a piercing truth: God resides not in caste, but in compassion and character.

Eventually, Chadheya and his wives recognize the divine beings, and his life is restored — a symbolic resurrection of both body and belief.

A Dance of Love, Struggles, and Social Norms

Chadheya Dance is not just a myth retold but a living metaphor for the cultural life of rural Ganjam. It portrays the love story between Chadheya and Chadeyani — lovers navigating societal expectations, familial consent, and traditional courtship.

Their romantic journey reflects the emotional and cultural fabric of Odisha's villages: from longing glances to moments of resistance, from collective rituals to community acceptance. The dance is a celebration of love that respects tradition yet quietly questions restrictive social codes.

Performance and Presentation

The dance is performed in vibrant synchrony by men and women, typically during Danda Yatra, weddings, and harvest celebrations. Male dancers (as Chadheya) wear dhotis or lungis, while female dancers (as Chadeyani) don traditional sarees, embodying elegance and rural authenticity.

Dancers form circles or lines, using energetic steps and expressive gestures to tell the story. Their movement is a visual poetry of emotions — from joy to devotion, from grief to divine realization.

Musical Rhythms and Folk Instruments

Chadheya Dance is brought to life with traditional Odia instruments like Dhol, Mardala, Chenda, and Khol. These create a pulsating rhythm that mirrors the emotional arcs of the narrative. Flutes and local songs enrich the performance with lyrical depth, turning each act into a melodic journey of longing, repentance, and reconciliation

Cultural and Spiritual Significance

Beyond its artistic value, Chadheya Dance plays a crucial role in community building and cultural continuity. It reinforces the values of family, mutual respect, and societal harmony. It subtly challenges casteism, while celebrating diversity and inclusivity through its storyline and characters.

It is also believed to have connections to the sacred temple of Lord Birupakhya in Fulbani and Chakapada, establishing a bridge between local belief systems and pan-Odisha spiritual traditions.

A Living Tradition That Speaks to Today

In a world still battling caste discrimination, environmental neglect, and eroding community bonds, the story of Chadheya resonates as an enduring message: Don't see the caste of people — choose humanity. Respect nature's course. Recognize the divine in the neglected.

The Chadheya Dance of Ganjam is not merely a dance — it is an artistic uprising, a philosophical dialogue, and a cultural embrace. It celebrates rural roots, mythological wisdom, and above all, the universal language of love and humanity.

Ghumura Dance of Kalahandi: A Vibrant Expression of Tribal Culture, Heroism, and Social Unity

The Ghumura Dance is one of the most dynamic and culturally rich folk dances originating from the Kalahandi district in Odisha, India. This dance form is deeply rooted in the region's tribal culture and is known for its energetic movements, distinct dress code, and bold, warrior-like style. It is traditionally performed by male dancers during significant festivals, community events, and rituals, particularly in the rural areas of Kalahandi. The Ghumura Dance continues to be an important cultural symbol of the region, showcasing the strength, unity, and spiritual devotion of the tribal people.

Origin and Tribal Roots:

The Ghumura Dance is believed to have its roots in the Indrāvati Peninsula, an area rich in tribal culture. It is primarily performed by the indigenous tribes of Kalahandi, such as the Gond, Bhatras, and Bhumia tribes, who are known for their distinct traditions and lifestyle. The dance serves as a vibrant expression of their cultural identity and is intrinsically linked to their community rituals and agricultural practices.

Key Features of Ghumura Dance:
1. Performance Style and Group Dance

The Ghumura Dance is a group dance, traditionally performed by a large number of dancers, ranging from 15 to 40 performers. It is usually performed by men, and the dance is marked by quick, energetic movements that often reflect the warrior-like demeanor of the tribal people. The dancers are in constant motion, performing coordinated footwork, vigorous arm movements, and bold gestures, often simulating the act of warfare or battle in their performance.

2. Tribal Attire and Dress Code

A key feature of the Ghumura Dance is its tribal dress code, which gives the performance a raw, traditional appeal. The dancers typically wear tribal attire, which includes dhotis or lungis, headgear made from natural materials like leaves or feathers, and sometimes shoulder ornaments or necklaces made from beads or other organic materials. This traditional dress symbolizes their connection to nature, and their warrior-like attire is a visual representation of the strength and resilience of the community.

3. Musical Accompaniment

The dance is accompanied by drums and other traditional percussion instruments, most notably the Ghumura drum. The Ghumura drum, which is the heart of the performance, provides the rhythmic foundation for the dancers. Other instruments such as dhols, flutes, and mardalas may also be played to complement the beat and add layers to the overall sound. The music is fast-paced and intense, fueling the energetic movements of the dancers.

4. Social and Cultural Significance

The Ghumura Dance is not only an expression of artistic tradition but also carries deep social significance. It is performed during major festivals such as Nuakhai (the harvest festival) and Dasahara, marking the seasonal celebrations and invoking blessings for a good harvest, prosperity, and protection from evil forces. The dance fosters social harmony, as it brings together members of the community in a collective celebration, reinforcing the bonds of kinship, friendship, and solidarity.

The dance also serves as a form of tribal unity, where different tribes and communities come together to showcase their shared cultural values. It plays an important role in community cohesion, as participants from different generations and backgrounds unite to perform and celebrate their heritage.

5. Cultural Representation and Regional Popularity

While the Ghumura Dance has traditionally been more prominent in the rural areas of Kalahandi, it has begun to gain wider recognition both within Odisha and beyond. The dance has represented Odisha at several international events, introducing people from different cultures to the rich tribal traditions of the region. The continued promotion and preservation of the Ghumura Dance have made it an iconic cultural representation of Odisha's tribal communities

The Role of Royal Families in Preserving the Dance:

Historically, royal families in Kalahandi have played a significant role in preserving and promoting the Ghumura Dance. Their patronage and support have helped ensure that the dance continues to be passed down through generations. The dance is not just a form of artistic

expression but also a way to preserve the cultural heritage and traditional values of the tribal people in Kalahandi.

The Ghumura Dance is much more than just a folk dance. It is a heroic celebration of the tribal people's strength, bravery, and unity. With its distinct attire, energetic performances, and musical accompaniment, it is an expression of the tribal identity of Kalahandi, deeply intertwined with the region's spiritual and agricultural practices. As the Ghumura Dance gains wider recognition, it continues to be a symbol of Odisha's tribal culture, promoting social unity and cultural pride.

Ghudki Dance: A Rhythmic Reflection of Western Odisha's Cultural Soul

Among the many vibrant folk traditions of India, the Ghudki dance—also known as Ghudka or Ghubukudu—stands out as a rhythmic and expressive folk art from Western Odisha, particularly the Sambalpuri region. Rooted deeply in the everyday life and cultural ethos of the people, Ghudki is more than just a dance—it is a celebration of identity, heritage, and community spirit.

Origins and Cultural Roots

The Ghudki dance originates from Western Odisha, a region known for its colorful Sambalpuri culture. It is especially associated with tribal and rural communities who have preserved this tradition through generations. The name "Ghudki" is derived from a unique folk percussion instrument that provides the dance with its signature rhythmic foundation.

Performers and Participation

Traditionally performed by men, the dance sometimes features female performers as well. Whether by local community members or professional folk troupes, the performance of Ghudki is often a communal experience, drawing both performers and audiences into its vibrant energy.

Music, Rhythm, and Movement

Central to the Ghudki dance is its music, characterized by traditional drums and percussive instruments. The rhythms are lively and dynamic, setting a pulsating pace for the dancers. Movements often mimic the gestures of animals or birds, drawing inspiration from daily life, nature, and local folklore. This naturalistic style creates a captivating visual narrative.

Themes and Storytelling

Beyond entertainment, Ghudki serves as a medium for storytelling. The themes may range from mythology and history to social customs and local legends. Like the Ghusadi dance of Telangana, it often incorporates symbolic movements and folk singing, reflecting the close connection between dance and oral tradition in Indian folk culture.

Cultural Significance

Ghudki is not merely a dance; it is a living tradition that allows people to celebrate festivals like Nuakhai Bhetghat, mark important social occasions, and foster a sense of belonging. Through its rhythmic expression, the dance reinforces cultural identity and social harmony within the community.

Preservation and Promotion

In recent years, efforts by institutions such as Odisha Tourism have aimed at promoting and preserving traditional art forms like Ghudki. Cultural festivals, exhibitions, and folk dance showcases have brought renewed attention to this valuable heritage, ensuring its transmission to newer generations.

The Ghudki dance, with its pulsating beats and expressive storytelling, remains a vital part of Western Odisha's cultural landscape. As both a symbol of tradition and a source of community pride, it continues to captivate audiences and remind us of the rich folk heritage of Odisha.

www.ingramcontent.com/pod-product-compliance
Lightning Source LLC
Chambersburg PA
CBHW060607080526
44585CB00013B/720